Columbia University

Contributions to Education

Teachers College Series

No. 632

AMS PRESS
NEW YORK

PHILOSOPHIES OF ADMINISTRATION CURRENT IN THE DEANSHIP OF THE LIBERAL ARTS COLLEGE

By Merle Scott Ward, Ph.D.

TEACHERS COLLEGE, COLUMBIA UNIVERSITY
CONTRIBUTIONS TO EDUCATION, No. 632

Published with the Approval of
Professor DONALD P. COTTRELL, *Sponsor*

BUREAU OF PUBLICATIONS
Teachers College, Columbia University
NEW YORK CITY
1934

Library of Congress Cataloging in Publication Data

Ward, Merle Scott, 1892-
    Philosophies of administration current in the
deanship of the liberal arts college.

    Reprint of the 1934 ed., issued in series:
Teachers College, Columbia University. Contributions
to education, no. 632.
    Originally presented as the author's thesis,
Columbia.
    Bibliography: p.
    1. Deans (in schools)--United States.
2. Universities and colleges--United States--
Administration. I. Title. II. Series: Columbia

University. Teachers College. Contributions to
education, no. 632.
    LB2341.W3 1972   378.1'12   79-177661
    ISBN 0-404-55632-9

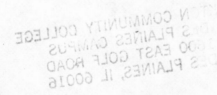

Reprinted by Special Arrangement with Teachers
College Press, New York, New York

From the edition of 1934, New York
First AMS edition published in 1972
Manufactured in the United States

AMS PRESS, INC.
NEW YORK, N. Y.   10003

Acknowledgments

WITH the publication of this study I wish to acknowledge my indebtedness to the many deans and other administrative officers of liberal arts colleges who so kindly furnished the information sought in the instruments.

To all teachers and students, in the various institutions visited, who have helped me to clearer thinking I tender my sincere thanks.

I wish especially to express my deep and genuine gratitude to Professor Helen Walker and Dr. Joseph Zubin for their valued counsel in regard to the statistical treatment of certain technical problems of the study, to Professor F. B. O'Rear for the many thought-provoking suggestions offered, to Professor R. B. Raup for the benefit of his wise counsel, and to Professor E. S. Evenden for the stimulus of his penetrating and indispensable criticisms.

Most of all, I am indebted to Professor D. P. Cottrell, my sponsor, whose keen thought, exhaustive thoroughness, and expert guidance throughout the entire period of the study were to me a constant stimulus and inspiration.

M. S. W.

New York City
June, 1934

Contents

Contents

Tables

PHILOSOPHIES OF ADMINISTRATION CURRENT IN THE DEANSHIP OF THE LIBERAL ARTS COLLEGE

CHAPTER I

Introduction

PRINCIPLES of administration in higher education can be appraised adequately only when the entire social situation is taken into account. The college is the product of society. It is an agent created by the social order to achieve certain definite objectives. Society defines these objectives, supplies the raw materials in terms of young men and young women, and furnishes the finances that sustain the institution. No matter how seclusive an institution of higher learning may desire to be, nor how completely it may wish to dissociate itself from its environment, it remains, nevertheless, part and parcel of the total social situation, and its obligations and responsibilities to society rest none the less lightly upon its shoulders as a result of its adverse aspiration. To determine, therefore, in any satisfactory measure, the purpose, organization, curriculum, activities, and principles of administration for a college or university requires first an analysis and understanding of the contemporary social scene.

Society today is in a ferment such as has not been known in our generation and perhaps not since the days of the Civil War. Economic and social practices that once went unchallenged are today tumbling into the discard. The very foundations of our economic system are shaking. Principles like "rugged individualism," old as the nation itself, prove no longer potent. Scientific inventions have transformed industry. Free land has disappeared. Production has reached a new high level until governmental authority intervenes to curtail it; yet men walk the streets hungry and find no useful remunerative task to perform. It is a day of solemn referendum on the creeds and practices of the older social order. They must be re-appraised in the light of the modern scene, and revised or discarded as impartial judgment determines.

In this total situation education plays a major rôle. It represents an abiding faith of the American Republic. Our people have established and supported through the years an educational system of singular completeness. In their democratic conception, this educational system is a ladder by which every boy and girl, regardless of birth, rank, or wealth, may climb through grades, high school, and university to the finest achievements of which they are capable. This, we have believed, would correct all evils. This was the agency designed to solve all problems. Today it stands bewildered and impotent in the midst of a merciless confusion.

Our people have regarded the college and university as the capstone of this educational system. The purposes of the early American college were cultural and vocational. These purposes were well expressed in the pamphlet, "New England's First Fruits," in these words:

. . . to advance learning and to perpetuate it to posterity, dreading to leave an illiterate ministry to the churches when our own present ministers shall lie in the dust.

Accordingly our ancestors formed an organization, adopted principles, and fashioned a curriculum designed to accomplish these purposes.

Today the scene is entirely changed. The higher institution of pre-Revolutionary days, outworn but not discarded, cannot hope through slight modification successfully to meet the demands of 1934. Yet in all too many instances youth of today are admitted to institutions of archaic organization and asked to give their attention to curricula and courses of study planned for their ancestors and perpetuated in this same early tradition.

Those who control and administer colleges and universities no longer can doubt that fundamental changes in the administration of higher education are imperative. Indeed, the widespread readjustments in the programs of many institutions indicate that this conclusion has already been reached by those in control. Frankly and courageously they have embarked upon "experiments." The results are yet to be appraised.

THE PURPOSE OF THIS STUDY

But to what extent have administrators of higher education as a whole accepted this conclusion, and how firm is their conviction therein? What do the deans of colleges, who have direct charge of the instructional program and who pàrticipate extensively in the administrative procedure—what do they think in regard to these controversial issues that now so sharply divide opinion in the whole field of higher education?

In this field of issues loom certain problems fraught with tremendous significance. Should the administration of a college conform wholeheartedly to the needs of students despite an increase in administrative difficulties, or should the students be forced to conform, without exception, to what officials may consider a well-ordered administration? Should the purpose of a liberal arts college, once appropriate to the needs of its contemporary society, generally remain permanent during the life of the institution even though society itself undergoes extensive change? Should a liberal arts college place chief emphasis upon the conservation and transmission of classical knowledge, or should it, instead, emphasize all experiences that would make for a fuller and better development of its students? Should the business pattern of control, with its principle of centralization of authority in a board and president, persist as the accepted form of organization and administration, or should the faculty and students participate in the formulation and execution of educational policies? Should a single definite social and economic doctrine, or the prevailing one, or all doctrines be presented through the curriculum and instruction of the institution? Is the curriculum to be considered sacrosanct and therefore immune to change, or should it be adapted, also, to the present needs of students of a new era? Are the instructional methods and practices on the college level best determined by the experience of effective college teachers, or is it essential that research and experimentation play their parts in the appraisal of these methods and practices? Is the present departmental plan the most effective educational organization for achieving the aims of liberal education, or should it be supplanted by the divisional or single unit plan? Are such innovations as student rating of instructors, homogeneous grouping, orientation courses, and observance of Freshman Week of real value to the college, or do they seem now to be generally undesirable? Is the furnishing to the student of a broad cultural background the only duty of the liberal arts college, or is it also charged with responsibilities for vocational guidance, placement, -

and follow-up of its graduates? Can the laissez-faire attitude toward higher education succeed indefinitely, or must there be a positive reorganization of higher education?

These and scores of other problems rise to trouble and perplex the college administrator of today. It is quite possible that the deans, as a group, are in the most strategic position of all educational leaders to direct and effect the reorganization of higher education. Certainly their influence would be distinctly felt in deliberations for that purpose. What the deans of liberal arts colleges are thinking, what educational philosophies they hold, what changes they are contemplating in the nature, offerings, and functions of their institutions are matters of prime importance today. It is chiefly to discover these facts, trends, and tendencies that this study has been essayed.

In order adequately to understand the present importance and influence of the deanship, it is necessary to know something of its origin, its development, the type of educator chosen to fill it, the duties he performs, and the philosophy that determines his decisions. This study has attempted, therefore, through available historical sources and through information furnished by 330 deans of liberal arts colleges in the United States, to trace the origin and development of the deanship; to determine its present status in the collegiate administrative scheme; to present, through personal and professional background data, an accurate picture of the present incumbent of the office; and to discover the opinions, controlling ideas and philosophies held by deans in their relation to four major areas of service, namely, (1) purpose of the college, (2) curriculum, (3) improvement of instruction, and (4) student welfare.

SOURCES AND TECHNIQUES

Approach to this problem through an historical sketch of the origin and development of the office of dean offers orientation values. The sources of data for this approach are of two types— historical documents and information from the present deans in the field.

The historical sources included the literature available on the origin and development of the deanship as contained in standard histories of the institutions, annual catalogues, annual reports of presidents, deans, and boards of directors, printed regulations, bulletins, newspapers and periodicals. The principal sources are included in the Bibliography of this study.

The raw data were secured from the liberal arts colleges of the United States as listed in the *Educational Directory* for 1933.[1]

To ascertain the opinions, preferences, judgments, and controlling ideas of deans of liberal arts colleges, it was found necessary to develop an instrument covering the major problems in the four areas previously designated. A detailed account of the construction of this instrument is given in Chapter II.

The historical questionnaire and instrument were further supplemented by Dr. D. P. Cottrell's "Test on Controversial Issues in Higher Education" (Revised Edition), which had been previously developed, revised, and standardized. The historical questionnaire, the instrument, and the "Test on Controversial Issues," are hereafter referred to by these respective titles.

Chapter III traces the origin and development of the deanship.

Chapter IV presents as complete a picture as possible of the personal and professional background of the present incumbents of the deanship in the liberal arts colleges of the United States.

Chapter V discusses the validity and reliability of the instruments and the construction of the scoring key.

Chapter VI presents an analysis and interpretation of the scores on the significant statements of the instrument, and the scores on the "Test on Controversial Issues in Higher Education." A comparative study is made of the responses in relation to age, sex, control, denomination, size of institution, character of student body, geographical location, racial nature of college, and philosophy of administration.

Chapter VII presents the conclusions drawn from the data gathered in this study.

Chapter VIII presents what the author believes is an emerging conception of the deanship, together with recommendations for reorganization of the office and for the betterment of educational practice in the liberal arts college.

PARTICIPATION OF INSTITUTIONS IN THE STUDY

The initial letter explaining the objectives of the study was addressed to deans of 622 four-year liberal arts colleges in the United

---

[1] U. S. Office of Education, *Educational Directory, 1933, Part III, Colleges and Universities.* Bulletin 1934, No. 1, pp. 72-111.

States, as listed in the *Educational Directory* for 1933.[2] Replies were received from 391 institutions, fifty-five of these stating they had no such office as dean of the college. The remaining 336 institutions forwarded returns. These returns consisted of the following: 336 historical questionnaires, six of which were found to be unusable; 332 instruments, two of these being unusable; 244 "Tests on Controversial Issues," seven being unusable.

Geographically, the returns represented every state in the United States, and the District of Columbia. They were likewise representative as to size of institution, control, and type of student body.

The list of coöperating institutions is given in Appendix A.

SUMMARY

A general view of the study as a whole has been briefly sketched in this introductory chapter. The problem has been outlined, the sources and techniques suggested, the plan of presentation of materials described, and the participation of institutions in the study summarized.

[2] *Op. cit.*, pp. 75-111.

CHAPTER II

Tools Used in Investigation

THE deans of the liberal arts colleges who participated in this study were requested to respond to three separate documents, namely, (1) an historical questionnaire on the origin and development of the office of dean in their respective institutions, (2) an instrument dealing with certain basic problems of college administration in four areas, of vital importance, and (3) the "Test on Controversial Issues."

The historical questionnaire and instrument were constructed specifically for this study and used initially therein. The "Test on Controversial Issues" was developed by Professor D. P. Cottrell, of Teachers College, Columbia University, in 1932, was administered to various groups of graduate students in Teachers College, and was revised to its present form in 1933.

THE HISTORICAL QUESTIONNAIRE

This brief document sought only pertinent data regarding the history of the deanship in the various institutions. It may be secured in the form in which it was used in this study from the author.

THE INSTRUMENT

In order to discover what deans of liberal arts colleges are thinking about certain crucial problems vitally related to the work of their offices, a particular type of instrument was deemed necessary. Such an instrument should include the salient issues in the major fields it proposed to cover, should permit ready expression of judgment by those participating, and should yield data that could be conveniently scored and effectively interpreted. For these purposes the multiple-choice type of statement was chosen and the task of building a suitable instrument was begun.

The literature of the field was combed in search of present crucial issues. The fact became readily apparent that all areas

7

of the dean's work could not be covered adequately within the limits of a questionnaire of reasonable length. Four vital fields, therefore, were selected, as follows: (1) purpose of the college, (2) curriculum, (3) improvement of instruction, and (4) student welfare.

A tentative list of multiple-choice statements, 166 in number, was then prepared and submitted to a jury consisting of members of the faculty of Teachers College and graduate students in the department of Higher Education of Teachers College. Elimination from this source reduced the number of statements to eighty-six. In this revised form the instrument was submitted for marking and criticism, during the 1933 Spring and Summer Sessions of Teachers College, successively to three groups, as follows: (1) seven members of the faculty of Teachers College; (2) ten graduate students in the department of Higher Education of Teachers College; (3) members of a class in a course called "The Work of the Dean of the Faculty," conducted by Professor D. P. Cottrell. This class was composed largely of deans of colleges widely scattered throughout the United States and was, therefore, considered a very valuable agency in the refinement of the instrument. During the summer of 1933 this experimental edition of the instrument was also submitted, for criticism and marking, to a large number of deans and members of faculties of fifteen different colleges in the Mid-west and Northwest.

Criticism by these groups was made, in writing, of the various statements and of the instrument as a whole, and was followed by interviews which proved particularly valuable. As a result of these numerous try-outs and conferences the instrument emerged in final form as a document of seventy-four multiple-choice statements and two ranking questions. These statements were preceded by a page for personal data essential to the proper interpretation of individual reactions. They were followed by a graphic self-rating scale on which the individual himself recorded the degree of his preference for the democratic or the autocratic conception of college administration, as defined in a preceding statement. By the use of this scale it was possible to devise a method of numerical scoring for each individual on the test. The construction of this scoring key is described in detail in Chapter V. The instrument may be secured in the form in which it was used in this study from the author.

"TEST ON CONTROVERSIAL ISSUES IN HIGHER EDUCATION"

To check and supplement this instrument, and also for its own valuable contribution, Dr. Cottrell's "Test on Controversial Issues in Higher Education" (Revised Edition) was included in the study. This test was constructed upon the hypothesis that individuals, in their appraisal of the worth of higher education, tend to be influenced in viewpoint predominantly by one of three basic philosophies, designated by the author as Classic-Centered, Professional-Centered, and Experience-Centered. These basic philosophies, in their relation to certain phases of higher education, were carefully defined and test items on major controversial issues within these areas were selected.[1]

This Experimental Edition included 180 controversial issues, represented by 162 multiple-choice and 18 ranking items. It was given in this preliminary form to 355 graduate students of Teachers College during the Summer Session of 1932. Of these graduate students, 77 were enrolled in courses in the professional field of Higher Education, 127 in Secondary Education, 41 in Educational Economics, and 110 in Student Personnel Administration. Report of the study for the group of 77 graduate students in the professional field of Higher Education was published in the *Teachers College Record* in May, 1933.

The Experimental Edition of the test was given, during the Winter, Spring, and Summer Sessions of 1932–1933, to successive classes conducted by Professor Cottrell. As a result of these tryouts it was subjected to critical revision. The Revised Edition was published in October, 1933, and was used as an instrument in this study. All ranking items were eliminated in the Revised Edition and the total number of items was reduced to 160.

The Revised Edition may be secured in the form in which it was used in this study from its author.

SUMMARY

This chapter has presented the tools used in this investigation and described in detail the method of their development. The extensive search for criticism and suggestions, and the meticulous care with which revisions were made in both the instrument and

[1] Cottrell, D. P., "The Measurement of Conflicting Viewpoints in Higher Education." *Teachers College Record*, Vol. XXXIV, pp. 635-54, May 1933.

the "Test on Controversial Issues" proved to be major factors in achieving validity and reliability for these documents. Since the instruments are new and comparatively unique, their validity and reliability will be discussed in detail in a later chapter.

The deans of 336 liberal arts colleges participated in the study by filling out these three documents. Their responses form the basis for the succeeding chapters.

CHAPTER III

Origin and Development of Deanship

WHILE a study of higher education in the United States today impresses one with the growing importance of the office of dean of the faculty, a review of the literature of American colleges reveals a discouraging dearth of material regarding its origin, development, and organization. Only by patient delving into the archives of institutions, perusal of minutes of boards of trustees, scanning of presidential reports, reports of other officials, institutional bulletins and documents can one piece together the haphazard course through which this office came to its present state in American collegiate institutions.

It should be stated at the outset that the office of college dean is by no means standardized even today. Its recency of origin, sporadic and haphazard development, and apparent lack of systematic thought as to its fundamental purposes are major contributing factors to the dilemma that exists at this time in regard to the deanship. As Dean Herbert E. Hawkes of Columbia College has aptly stated:

There is, however, no such thing as a standardized dean. There is the dean of this and that college, but I never have seen any two deans who could exchange places and retain the same duties.[1]

The present chaos in the functional organization of the office is aptly illustrated by Professor Irwin J. Lubbers, whose survey of current practices in 180 independent liberal arts colleges in the United States prompted him to write:

The situation of some Deans, perhaps their number is considerable, is similar to that in one of the larger colleges under consideration. After having dismissed, to the embarrassment of the interviewer, all questions regarding institutional administration with the repeated statement that they were no concern of his, he arose and pleasantly bade his visitor good day and terminated the interview with this observation, "and if you can some

[1] Hawkes, H. E., "College Administration," *Journal of Higher Education,* Vol I, p. 245, May 1930.

day tell me what the duties of a Dean are, I shall be truly grateful." This Dean was an elderly gentleman who had served the college long and well and as an author had reflected much credit upon the institution which he served.[2]

DERIVATION AND EARLY USES OF TITLE

In view of these related facts it seems timely to study the origin and development of the deanship. As a point of departure it is interesting to note the derivation of the word "dean" and its applications in ancient days. President Charles F. Thwing has suggested that the term was "borrowed from the church."[3]

Records, however, reveal that the title was in use long before the church employed it. The term is derived from the Greek "seka" and the Latin "decanus," meaning "ten." It was probably originally used to denote a military grade. Such use was made of it in the *De Re Militari of Vegetius*, written in A.D. 386. The ancient codes of Theodosius and Justinian mentioned "deans" as officers of the Roman civil administration. Primarily the term was employed to designate "one having authority over ten." In this fashion, in A.D. 400, St. Jerome used the term in the Vulgate in preference to "decurio," which was the old Latin version.

From the fourth century on it came to be used in many types of activities and for various designations. It was applied to members of a guild whose occupation was the burial of the dead, to certain minor officials of the imperial household, and later to various civil functionaries in the Roman Empire. Codes of the Visigoths and Lombards reveal that the title was applied among these peoples to a subordinate judge who had jurisdiction within a district called a "decania" or deanery. The Anglo-Saxons used the title in a corresponding way, interchanging the words "dean," "tithing-man," and "head-borough."

The church very early in its history borrowed the term, applying it first in the monasteries. There a "decanus" was appointed over every ten monks, to have charge of their discipline. When canonical life was introduced among the clergy attached to the cathedrals, the title came to be applied to the head of the chapter. It has continued to be used by certain religious bodies ever since.

---

[2] Lubbers, Irwin J., *College Organization and Administration*, p. 81.
[3] Thwing, Charles F., "College Presidents: Whence They Come, Whither Do They Go, What Do They Do?" *School and Society*, Vol. XXXV, p. 3, Jan. 2, 1932.

In Germany today deans of chapters, with executive and sometimes secular functions, are appointed by the bishop or chapter. In England deans of cathedrals are appointed by the crown. In addition, there are "deans of peculiars," such as Westminster, Windsor, Bocking, and Croydon, and rural deans whose duties are to visit the parishes and report to the bishop. In the United States rural deans are known as deans of convocation, the title being used in some dioceses of the American Episcopal Church. Their functions have not been clearly defined.

The title of dean early appeared in many of the great modern universities of Europe. At Oxford and Cambridge the office was established to superintend discipline. One exception to this practice exists at Oxford, where the dean of Christ Church, which is both cathedral and college, is the head of the college. In this particular office, therefore, are found both administrative and disciplinary functions. Usually, though, in the colleges of the English universities one of the fellows holds the office of dean and is responsible for discipline as distinguished from the regular teaching function of the tutor. The President of the Scottish Faculty of Advocates is called Dean of the Faculty, and in some universities the head of the faculty is given that title.

In German universities it is the practice for the faculty to elect a dean annually. The dean then presides over the meetings of the faculty, represents it in its external relations, and supervises both faculty and student body.

In addition to the disciplinary and administrative types of deans, there is a third fashion in which the title has been applied. The oldest member in length of service in a group of equal rank has, in various organizations, been designated as dean. The senior Cardinal Bishop in the Roman Catholic Church, who always occupies the see of Ostia, is Dean of the Sacred College. He presides, in the absence of the Pope, over the deliberations of the Sacred College and at coronation proceedings. The oldest member of the diplomatic corps at a national capital, in point of service at that capital, is usually recognized as dean. Other miscellaneous uses of the term, embodying one or more of the functional phases of the office, are found in the offices of presidents of incorporated bodies of lawyers and in the executive offices of trade guilds and other forms of trade associations.

THREE TYPES OF DEANS IN AMERICAN COLLEGES

From this heterogeneous application of the term "dean" the title was carried to American higher education. Having no single definite application abroad, it came likewise to serve indiscriminate purposes in this country. Three definite types of deans have appeared in higher education in the United States. These three types are: (1) dean by virtue of seniority, (2) dean of men or women, and (3) academic dean or dean of the faculty. The derivation of all three types is clearly found in ancient European practices in civil, religious, and educational institutions.

The first type—dean by virtue of seniority—is substantially honorary. Its persistent hold on the administration of higher education in the United States is evident even today. The survey of 180 independent liberal arts colleges, made by Irwin J. Lubbers, revealed that

in 25% of the colleges the Deans are men who have earned the right to an honorary title and the impression persists, despite its subjective nature, that the office of Dean is used for the purpose of bestowing that honor.[4]

Reeves and Russell, in their survey of thirty-five Methodist liberal arts colleges, corroborated Lubbers' findings and pertinently suggested another dangerous basis of appointment to this office:

In many of the colleges the dean is one of the older members of the faculty. Appointment to this office, while not exactly a matter of seniority, has tended in such colleges to be limited to teachers long associated with the institution. In a few colleges the choice of a dean has been influenced by teaching loads, the theory being that a teacher with a small load will have more time for the administrative duties of the deanship. The person assigned this office in such colleges will typically be a member of a department which attracts relatively few students.[5]

The second type of dean—dean of men or women—developed in American institutions out of the old European religious and educational concept of an officer in charge of discipline.

The University of Illinois is commonly credited with leading the way in the creation of this office, having definitely established it in 1901.[6]

The first incumbent was Thomas Arkle Clark, who served in

---

[4] Lubbers, *op. cit.*, p. 81.

[5] Reeves, F. W. and Russell, J. D., *The Liberal Arts College*, p. 86.

[6] Clark, Thomas Arkle, "The History and Development of the Office of Dean of Men," *School and Society*, Vol. XVI, p. 66, July 15, 1922.

that capacity for more than a quarter of a century and by his distinguished service wrote his name large in the annals of college administrative history. He himself, however, disclaims the distinction generally accorded him of being the first dean of men in an American college. In 1922, in preparation for the writing of his brief history of the office, he addressed some thirty letters to deans of men in as many prominent institutions in the United States, requesting information relative to the establishment of the office in their respective colleges and universities. The only reply that indicated establishment of the office prior to 1901 was from Dean John Straub of the University of Oregon, who wrote:

There is the office of dean of men at the University of Oregon and I am "it." . . . The office was theoretically established in 1878 when I first came here and while I was not officially dean of men at that time, I acted in that capacity from that day until this, and part of that time I was also dean of women, which was a very pleasant duty.[7]

Dean Clark's own appointment, in 1901, to the office at the University of Illinois is humorously described by him in these words:

One morning early in the fall of 1900, I was called to the president's office. When I was ushered in I found him seated opposite a young fellow who had been registered in the University during the previous year but whose intellectual assets as indicated on the books of the University aggregated two hours of military and one in physical training. He was starting this second year with about the same enthusiasm as formerly, and the president was at his wit's end. The boy was the son of a prominent citizen of the state whose influence in the support and progress of the institution could not be ignored, but the president's self-respect would not let him keep the boy unless a change could be brought about.

Bob would not go to class, he would not study, and rumor had it that his habits were pretty unsavory.

When I came into the room there were indications of a recent hot conflict of words between the two, though just at that moment silence had fallen upon them.

"I'm through with this loafer," the president said to me. "If he won't change his habits, he will have to go home. I'm going to see what you can do with him. Whatever you do will be satisfactory to me. If he won't work, send him home."

I suppose I was dean of men from that time on, though I balked for a long time at the thought of taking the job over officially; but I solved Bob's difficulty that year, helped him to get on his feet, and made a friend of him for life, besides rescuing a high class first baseman from the intellectual scrap heap and so helping to win a championship. . . . I presume it was

[7] Clark, *op. cit.*, p. 66.

some such situation or crisis as I have described which has been responsible for the creation of the office in every institution.[8]

The third type of deanship—dean of the faculty—is largely a product of the twentieth century. Instances, indeed, of its establishment prior to 1900 are on record, but it was not until the twentieth century, with its spectacular increase in college enrollments, was reached, that the office took on a fairly universal aspect.

In the days of small enrollments the president of the college handled all problems of the faculty and student body. So long as the institution was small and the financial pressure comparatively light, the early college president struggled on alone, discharging a multitude of duties and solving all types of problems. Administratively, the college then was a one-man institution, with occasional slight assistance from clerical help and faculty committees.

With the turn of the twentieth century, and the accompanying large increases in enrollments, which, in turn, created the necessity for additional funds, executives and governing boards found it no longer possible for the president to handle all the details of administration. The financial need became the dominant one, requiring that the president go out into the field to make wider contacts and raise larger funds. In his absence some one must carry on the duties too pressing to be postponed. The president, therefore, began to delegate certain functions to members of the staff, to committees, or to other officers of the college. Gradually this process widened and out of these delegated functions arose the office of dean of the faculty.

In institutions conducted by the Society of Jesus, the office of Prefect of Studies almost invariably existed from their founding. This is the ancient office of "Praefectus Studiorum," dating from the "Ratio Studiorum" in 1599.[9] This office corresponded very closely to the present office of dean, since the prefect of studies was the chief assistant to the rector or president and in charge of all classes and supervision. Generally it included most duties now discharged by dean, registrar, dean of men, and other specialized offices.

Such a prefect of studies existed at Fordham University from

---

[8] Clark, *op. cit.*, pp. 66f.

[9] Fitzpatrick, Edward A., *St. Ignatius and the Ratio Studiorum*, (tr. of "Ratio Atque Institutio Studiorum Societatis Jesu," Neapoli, 1599), pp. 142-50.

its founding in 1841, the title being changed to dean in 1919. St. Joseph's College, at Philadelphia, established the office at its founding in 1851, changing to the modern term in 1917. The office of prefect of studies at the University of Santa Clara dates from the institution's founding in 1851, at Niagara University from its founding in 1856, and at St. Viator College, at Bourbonnais, Illinois, from its founding in 1868. Other American colleges conducted by the Society of Jesus, such as Gonzaga University of Spokane, Rosary College of River Forest, Illinois, St. John's University of Brooklyn, St. Peter's College of Jersey City, New Jersey, and Xavier University of Cincinnati, had the office of prefect of studies from their founding, changing later to the more modern title.

FIRST DEANSHIP AT HARVARD

The first officer to hold the title of Dean of the Faculty in a collegiate institution in the United States, so far as available historical sources and information from 336 deans in the field reveal, was appointed by President Eliot at Harvard in 1870.[10] It was the first year of his presidency of that institution. He had been a member of the faculty and had observed the effect of too-onerous duties on the executive. Members of the governing boards of Harvard had made a similar observation. Upon President Eliot's suggestion, early in his first year as executive, the new office of Dean of the College Faculty was established by statute, and Professor Ephraim W. Gurney, of the History Department, became the first officer to hold that title in American collegiate history.

The Forty-fifth Annual Report of the President of Harvard College, for the year 1869–1870, which was President Eliot's first report, carried the following important item:

Appointments (unlimited or for terms longer than one year) Ephraim W. Gurney, Professor of History, to be Dean of the College Faculty, January 28, 1870.[11]

Later in the body of the report the reasons for creating the office are given and the duties assigned to the appointee are thus defined:

The discussion which preceded and accompanied the last election of President of the University showed clearly that both the Governors and the

[10] Eliot, Charles W., *Forty-fifth Annual Report of Harvard College*, p. 4.
[11] Eliot, *op. cit.*, p. 4.

Alumni thought that the President had too much to do, and that he should be relieved of the immediate charge of the College administration. To carry into effect this universal opinion, the Corporation and Overseers, in the months of January and February, 1870, concurred in adopting a new statute creating the new office of Dean of the College Faculty, and defining the duties of the Dean. These statutes are as follows:

"The Dean of the College Faculty is appointed by the Corporation, with the consent of the Board of Governors, from among the members of the Faculty. It is his duty to preside at the meetings of the Faculty in the absence of the President; to administer the discipline of the College; to take charge of all petitions from undergraduates to the Faculty; to keep the records of admission and matriculation; to furnish such lists of students as may be required by the Faculty or the several teachers; to prepare all scales of scholarship, and preserve the records of conduct and attendance; to submit each year to the Faculty lists of persons to be recommended for scholarships and beneficiary aid, and likewise a list of those who appear, from the returns made to his office, to have complied with all the regular conditions for the degree of Bachelor of Arts; and in general to superintend the clerical and administrative business of the College."

The new office was immediately filled by the appointment of Professor E. W. Gurney, a gentleman singularly fitted both by nature and by experience to discharge the delicate and important duties of the place. It is wisely provided that the Dean shall be a professor, for the duties of the office can be much better performed by one who becomes acquainted with all the students by meeting them in the class-room, than by one who sees them only when they have business with him. The creation of this office is a great improvement in the organization of the University. The College is better administered than ever before and the other departments of the University can have a fairer share of the President's time and thought. The Dean has a very responsible and laborious office. He is at the head of the most highly organized and vigorous department of the University, and has charge at this moment of more students than were found in the whole University twenty years ago. He may have a strong personal influence over many young men with whom he necessarily becomes more or less intimate. He does three-quarters of the work which used to be done by the President. The Corporation have done what they could to recognize the dignity of the office by fixing the salary at forty-five hundred dollars a year.[12]

It is interesting to follow the development of the office of dean through the presidential reports of President Eliot. In his report on January 8, 1875, for the college year 1874–1875, is found this significant reference:

When the office of Dean of the Faculty was first created six years ago, there were 563 students in College. There are now 776, an increase of 38%. Within the same period the elective system has been greatly enlarged, while

[12] Eliot, *op. cit.*, pp. 11 f.

prescribed work has proportionally diminished; and this change has materially increased the work to be done in the Dean's office. In order to relieve the Dean, as far as possible, of the routine work of the office, and so to make it practicable for a professor actively engaged in teaching to hold this important office, the Corporation have enlarged the duties and increased the compensation of the Registrar of the College Faculty, and have confided to this officer construction, of all scales of rank, conduct of ordinary business with students, preparation of routine business for the Faculty, supervision of records of absence, direction of admission examinations and charge of other details which, with all matters just specified, have heretofore been regarded as in the province of the Dean. This measure took effect at the beginning of the current year.[13]

Dean Gurney served in that capacity for six years, resigning in January, 1876. President Eliot paid tribute to his first Dean of the College Faculty in these words:

In January, 1876, Professor Gurney resigned the office of Dean of the Faculty, which he had held for six years, and received leave of absence from the duties of professor, that he might make a somewhat prolonged stay in Europe. Professor Gurney was the first incumbent of the Dean of the Faculty, an office created in 1870. He contrived its methods, established its precedents, and set its standards. To the discharge of his new and often delicate functions, Professor Gurney brought ready tact and insight, unfailing courtesy and uncommon firmness, much experience and a quick and sound judgment—qualities and resources which every day's work brought effectively into play. It is the unanimous opinion of the governing boards and his colleagues that, by his skillful, and successful conduct of a new and growing department of administration, Professor Gurney rendered to the College a service which will be of lasting worth. The six annual reports which Professor Gurney made as Dean cover the period when the College was changing and growing fast; they treat, either briefly or at length, of most topics which governors of American colleges have in these days to consider,—such as extension of the elective system, students' choice of studies, system of honors, proper studies preparatory to college, separation of scales of conduct and scholarship, and voluntary attendance at recitations and lectures. These reports are in themselves clear, thoughtful, and cogent; but it greatly enhances their value that they are the work, not of a theorist or critic merely, but of one who wrote under responsibility, and was daily taking action about the matters he discussed.[14]

Upon the resignation of Dean Gurney there seems to have been no thought on the part of the administration of discontinuing the office. It had proved its worth and won a permanent place in the Harvard University organization. The same annual report of

---

[13] Eliot, Charles W., *Fiftieth Annual Report of Harvard College*, p. 17.
[14] *Ibid.*, pp. 4f.

President Eliot that carried the preceding tribute to Dean Gurney contained the following item under the heading of "appointments":

Charles F. Dunbar, to be Dean of the College, January 10, 1876.[15]

The annual reports of Dean Gurney to the president for the six years he held that office are replete with information as to the areas of his work and the specific duties he performed. The first report, for the college year 1869–1870, discusses the following topics:

1. Number of students enrolled by classes
2. Courses of instruction
3. Curriculum offerings
4. Examinations
5. Discipline
6. Bestowing of college honors
7. Admissions
8. Electives
9. Changes in program of courses
10. Announcement of program of courses for following year
11. Assignment of rooms in college dormitories
12. Need of recitation rooms and equipment
13. Decision of faculty that hereafter discipline and scholarship scales are to be kept apart.[16]

The succeeding five annual reports follow practically the same outline, with here and there an addition as new problems arose. The advance of the elective system at Harvard can be traced distinctly in these reports, as can the enrollment, curriculum and instructional developments.

EARLY DEANSHIPS IN OTHER COLLEGES

At Lincoln University, in Pennsylvania, Rev. E. R. Bower, who previously had been designated "Clerk of the Faculty," was, in 1871, elected by the faculty to the office of "Dean of the Faculties of Arts and Theology." No mention is made of this act in the presidential report to the board of trustees, explanation for which probably lies in the fact that at that time the deanship was an elective office on the part of the faculty.

The office of "Dean of Liberal Arts" was established at Syracuse University at its organization in 1873. In 1876 the chief

15 *Ibid.,* p. 5.
16 Gurney, E. W., *Report of Dean of College Faculty to President of Harvard College,* January, 1871.

executive officer of Fisk University was given the title of "Dean of the Faculty." This action was taken because of a three-year absence of the newly-elected president from the university. Howard University, at Washington, D. C., established the office of dean in June, 1877. Increase in the administrative burdens of the vice-provost of the University of Pennsylvania led to the establishment of the deanship as a separate office at that institution in 1877. The University of Nebraska and the University of Southern California established the office in 1880. Marquette University and the University of Detroit followed the trend in 1881. Princeton University established the office in 1883 to relieve the president of too-onerous duties. The year 1884 found the deanship established at Findlay College, Haverford College, and Yale College. At the opening of Bryn Mawr in 1885 the deanship was created, in the words of the present dean,

for Miss M. Carey Thomas, who was appointed in order to have the general advice and guidance of the whole body of students and also to make a study of the academic needs of the College. The office went out of existence for a number of years when Miss Thomas became the President of the College, but it was revived in 1907 and Miss Marion Reilly was appointed to it. At first she acted chiefly as the adviser of students but the office has developed naturally and now bears the responsibility for most of the routine academic administration, and the Dean is also responsible for the general supervision and study of the curriculum.[17]

DATES OF ESTABLISHMENT OF DEANSHIPS

By 1885 fifteen deanships had been established in the 319 liberal arts colleges furnishing these particular data in this study. The dates of the establishment of the office in these institutions, as reported by their respective deans, are presented in Appendix B.

In a large number of instances, in reporting these dates, reference was made by the dean to documentary evidence, such as the minutes of the board of trustees, minutes of the faculty, presidential reports, reports of deans, catalogues, and other publications of the institutions. Often this evidence was quoted on the historical questionnaire returned in this study. Available publications of the institution frequently confirmed the report of the dean.

It is evident from the data presented in Appendix B that the deanship is a comparatively recent development in American

---

[17] Personal letter from Mrs. Helen Taft Manning, Dean of the College, Bryn Mawr College, Bryn Mawr, Pennsylvania, dated December 4, 1933.

higher education. The range in the dates of the founding of these 319 institutions is 297 years, while the range in the dates of the establishment of deanships is only 63 years. The median date for the founding of these same institutions is 1871. The median date for the establishment of the deanship is 1913. These data are presented in full in Table 1.

TABLE 1

DATES OF THE FOUNDING AND OF THE ESTABLISHMENT OF THE DEANSHIP IN 319 COLLEGES

Year	Number of Colleges Founded	Number of Deanships Established
1636–1869	152	0
1870–1874	21	3
1875–1879	12	3
1880–1884	22	8
1885–1889	26	9
1890–1894	19	22
1895–1899	11	14
1900–1904	8	33
1905–1909	7	34
1910–1914	12	56
1915–1919	11	51
1920–1924	10	43
1925–1929	6	29
1930–1933	2	14
Total	319	319
Median year	1871	1913

CIRCUMSTANCES LEADING TO CREATION OF DEANSHIP

The circumstances leading to the creation of the office of dean in 330 liberal arts colleges included in this study were many and varied. Frequently the deanship was established to aid the president, as at Princeton, Harvard, and Indiana University. Sometimes it was developed to meet an emergency, such as illness, resignation or death of the president, as at Centre College, Connecticut College, and the College of Puget Sound. Often it came about through the reorganization of the institution, as at Alabama College and Mount Union College, in Ohio. In many instances it was created at the opening of the college, as at Cornell University, the University of Chicago, and the American University, at Washington, D. C. In the greatest number of cases, however, it was a logical step in the natural development of the institution.

In all, thirty-six different reasons were assigned by 289 institutions of the 330 reporting. These thirty-six reasons, with

TABLE 2

CIRCUMSTANCES LEADING TO ESTABLISHMENT OF OFFICE OF DEAN IN
330 COLLEGES

Circumstances Leading to Establishment of Deanship	Number of Colleges Assigning Cause
Natural development of institution	102
Established at opening of college	48
To aid the president	27
Reorganization of the college	18
President frequently absent	10
Need of better system	9
President busy soliciting money	8
Advent of new president	8
Resignation of president	5
Temporary president appointed dean	5
In order to have same title as sister institutions	5
Illness of president	4
An adviser of students needed	4
Organization on four-year college basis	3
To have some one in charge of discipline	3
In order to conform to custom	3
Retiring president made dean	2
To meet demand of accrediting agencies	2
Need of some one to deal with internal problems of administration	2
Reorganization into distinct liberal arts college	2
For the welfare of the students	2
Registrar's work had to be divided	2
To handle personnel problems	2
Sudden death of president	1
Retirement of president approaching	1
To fill temporary presidential vacancies	1
Merging of institutions	1
To centralize discipline and faculty leadership	1
Recognition of work covering many years	1
Progressive idea of new president	1
President requested vice-president be made dean	1
Title changed from "Secretary" to "Dean of College"	1
Honorary title to senior member of faculty	1
Incorporated as college in Commonwealth of Pennsylvania	1
To raise standards and efficiency of college	1
A separate woman's college established	1
Cause unknown	41

the number of liberal arts colleges assigning them, are listed in Table 2.

VARIED ORIGINS OF DEANSHIP

The deanship, likewise, developed from a variety of offices. Often the vice-presidency was changed into a deanship, as at Carthage College, Earlham College, and Livingstone College, in North Carolina. Frequently it developed from a faculty committee, as at the University of North Dakota, West Virginia University, and the University of Arkansas. Frequently, too, it developed from the office of registrar, as at Carroll College, Eureka College, and Butler University. In some instances it arose from the post of secretary of the college, as at Vassar, Norwich University, and the University of Arizona. Most frequently it was created outright, which was the case at Dartmouth, State College of Washington, and the University of Florida.

The various offices from which the deanship arose in the institutions participating in this study are listed in Table 3, together with the number of instances, respectively, among the institutions furnishing information on this item.

Such is the record of the emergence of the deanship in American educational history. Today more than three-fourths of the colleges and universities in the United States have a college dean or dean of the faculty. In a survey, made in 1930, of 180 independent liberal arts colleges scattered throughout the United States, Lubbers found the office of dean of the college in 127, or 71 per cent.[18]

In a recent study of 116 liberal arts colleges in the United States, Kinder found 104 (90 per cent) had the office of dean. Of the remaining twelve, seven were temporary vacancies and five were permanent.[19]

In the present study of 391 colleges and universities, the office of dean was found in 330, or 84.4 per cent. It is rarely found in colleges of less than 100 enrollment. In colleges of this size the work of the dean is usually handled through the president's office. The movement to establish the office in institutions of larger enrollments is still proceeding, though at a much slower pace than during the 1910–1920 decade. Figures of recent studies indicate that the saturation point has about been reached. There

[18] Lubbers, *op. cit.,* p. 81.
[19] Kinder, J. S., *The Internal Administration of the Liberal Arts College,* p. 25.

TABLE 3

OFFICES FROM WHICH DEANSHIP DEVELOPED IN 330 COLLEGES

Office from Which Deanship Developed	Number of Colleges Assigning Origin
Created outright	167
Vice-president	33
Faculty committee	26
Registrar	23
Secretary	9
Prefect of studies	9
Chairman of faculty	8
Secretary of faculty	4
Principal	4
Department head	3
Assistant to president	3
Lady principal	3
Head of Department of Education	2
Director of admission and credits	2
Directress of academy	2
Educational secretary to the president and director of research	1
Chief executive officer	1
Secretary of faculty and dormitory proctor	1
"Governor"	1
Senior class officer	1
Dean of women	1
President	1
Acting president	1
Class tutor	1
Vice-provost	1
Vice-president and advisory committee	1
Vice-chancellor	1
Treasurer and head of Department of Humanities	1
Business manager	1
Board of deans	1
Chairman of board of class deans	1
Dean of men	1
Chairman of Freshman advisers	1
Enrolling officer	1
Unknown	13

are occasional instances, as at Colgate University and Intermountain Union College in Montana, where the office has been discontinued, usually because of the demand for financial retrenchment. On the whole, however, it may be concluded that the deanship has come to be generally accepted as a necessary and essential administrative office in higher education.

But the office itself is still in the process of development. In few institutions even at this date is it adequately organized or its duties definitely defined. Kinder reports that in 55 per cent of 90 liberal arts colleges studied in his survey, no definition of the duties of the several administrative offices had been made.[20]

All stages of evolution of the deanship can be found among the colleges. In some it has not yet been established; in a number it has been combined with the office of dean of men; in still others it has been combined with the office of registrar. Reeves and Russell report that at the time the data for their study were being gathered "the offices of dean and registrar were held by a single individual in approximately one-half of the institutions."[21]

Kinder found that the dean also held another administrative title in 29 (28%) of the 116 institutions studied, as follows: registrar—17, dean of men—7, vice-president—2, librarian—2, and college pastor—1.[22]

The tendency seems to be toward combination of the offices of dean and registrar in the smaller colleges and toward subordination of the office of registrar to that of dean in the larger institutions. Kinder found, in 104 colleges and universities of which only 15 were 1,000 or more in enrollment, that 13 registrars (11%) were directly responsible to the dean and 5 (4%) were directly responsible to the dean and president.[23] Lubbers found that in 47 institutions (26%) out of 180 the registrar was directly responsible to the dean.[24]

Not only does the dean frequently discharge duties of other administrative officers, but in a very large percentage of the cases he does actual teaching. This is particularly true in the smaller institutions. Kinder found, in his study of 116 liberal arts colleges, that 90 per cent of the deans were doing some teaching. A number of them, in the smaller colleges, were teaching more than sixteen hours, which is the maximum set by standardizing agencies for full-time instructors without administrative duties. The median teaching load for deans in the group of 104 colleges (101 of which were less than 1,000 in enrollment) was eight hours. In 7 of the 11 largest institutions (over 1,000 in enroll-

---

[20] Kinder, *op. cit.*, pp. 45f.
[21] Reeves, F. W. and Russell, J. D., *College Organization and Administration*, p. 70.
[22] Kinder, *op. cit.*, p. 56.
[23] *Ibid.*, p. 60.
[24] Lubbers, *op. cit.*, p. 2.

ment) the deans were teaching, but carried a lighter teaching load.[25]

So far as actual classroom teaching by deans is concerned, there is much in its favor and little to be said against it. The point to be emphasized is that the time of the dean must be safeguarded to the extent that so much is not required by this particular duty as to prejudice his functioning in other vital and essential fields. It is obvious that a teaching load of sixteen hours or over is excessive for one who has the duties of the deanship to discharge.

In the haphazard development of the deanship, it was only natural that many incongruities would creep into the organization of the office. That they have done so is a matter of record. Reeves and Russell, after studying the administrative organization of thirty-five Methodist Episcopal liberal arts colleges, conclude as follows:

The results of this study indicate the probability that, if enough colleges were visited, the range of duties performed by each of the major officers would be found to include the total scope of administrative responsibilities. In other words, if enough colleges are included, the deans will be found to be doing everything done by any administrative officer; the same will be true for the president, the registrar, and the business manager.[26]

Kinder's study verifies this prediction, so far as the dean is concerned. An aggregate of sixty functions of all the administrative offices combined was prepared and submitted for marking to the deans of 116 liberal arts colleges. Tabulation revealed that the dean of the college in one college or another performed all sixty of the functions listed.[27]

In institutions where the office of dean has existed for a considerable period of time, its duties have generally increased in scope. Expansion, indeed, has been so great that some of the duties performed earlier by the dean are now being delegated to new or subordinate officers as additional vital responsibilities present themselves at the dean's door.

The dean of the faculty is in a strategic position in relation to many of the major problems in higher education today. Increasingly he is becoming the head of college instructional administration. Improvement of instruction, personnel work, admissions,

[25] Kinder, op. cit., pp. 25, 40, 42.
[26] Reeves, F. W. and Russell, J. D., The Liberal Arts College, p. 86.
[27] Kinder, op. cit., pp. 50-53.

student counseling, comprehensive examinations, honors courses, curriculum revision, clarification of the purpose of the college, experimentation of various types—all these and other fields are open to the dean who wills and dares to exercise his leadership.

The office is still in evolution. Expansion continues, and with it new opportunities for distinguished service present themselves. Lubbers writes:

Of all major offices, that of Dean enjoys the best prospect of growing in influence and prestige.[28]

That growth depends primarily (1) upon the proper definition of the duties and responsibilities of the office, and (2) upon the type of leaders chosen to exercise its functions.

SUMMARY

The origin and development of the office of dean of the faculty in the American liberal arts college have been traced briefly in this chapter. Data have revealed the office to be of comparatively recent development in American higher education, yet to date practically 85 per cent of the liberal arts colleges in the United States have established the office. The dates of the establishment of the deanship in 319 institutions, as reported by the deans of these colleges and universities, are listed in Appendix B.

Developing out of a variety of offices and from differing and often peculiar circumstances, the deanship has consequently lacked uniformity of organization. Concise definition of authority, duties, and responsibilities is sorely needed before deans generally can realize fully on their possibilities for accomplishment in higher education.

[28] Lubbers, *op. cit.*, p. 144.

CHAPTER IV

Background of the College Dean

THE office of dean of the faculty in the liberal arts college has attained to date no appreciable degree of standardization. In this anomalous situation the type of individual who holds the office is a fruitful source for study, for his personality will color and his philosophy largely determine the activities of the deanship. Dean Carl E. Seashore, of the University of Iowa, has written:

> It is likely that personal interests and aptitudes determine in large part what a dean shall do or not do and it is probably wholesome that an officer's personality shall color the activities of the office in such a way as to retain and foster natural interests and not cover up the human element in the situation.[1]

In short, the power of the dean very largely may be just what his personality, knowledge, and abilities can make it. It is therefore essential to know something of the background of the individual who occupies the deanship in the liberal arts college.

AGE, SEX, AND RACE OF COLLEGE DEANS

Table 4 shows that deans generally are mature individuals. Only 3 in the total group (1%) are under 30 years of age, and only 52 (15.7%) are under 40 years of age. The large majority, 212 (64.2%), are between the ages of 40 and 60, while 66 (20%) are 60 years of age or over. It is evident that liberal arts colleges do not ordinarily choose their deans from the lower age levels.

The age range (from 25 to 68) and median age (49) for women deans differ considerably from those for deans of women in land-grant institutions. In the study of thirty-nine deans of women in land-grant institutions, in 1927, Miss Madge McGlade found their ages to range from under 30 to 45 or above, with the median at 45.[2]

---

[1] Seashore, Carl E., "The Dean's Office," *Fifty Years of Progress*, 1925.
[2] Office of Education, *Survey of Land-Grant Colleges and Universities*, Bulletin No. 9, 1930, p. 406.

TABLE 4

AGE OF 330 COLLEGE DEANS IN RELATION TO SEX AND RACE

Age	SEX		RACE		Total
	Male	Female	White	Negro	
20–29	2	1	3	0	3
30–39	43	6	40	9	49
40–49	93	19	107	5	112
50–59	85	15	97	3	100
60–69	52	6	56	2	58
70–79	7	0	7	0	7
80–89	1	0	1	0	1
Total	283	47	311	19	330
Age Range	53	43	56	31	56
Median age	50	49	50	40	50

Deans of Negro colleges tend to be younger than deans of White colleges. In the nineteen Negro colleges included in this study 9 deans (47.3%) are under 40 years of age, while only 43 (13.8%) deans of White colleges are under 40 years of age. The reason for this difference may be found in the shorter educational experience of the Negro race at the college level.

TABLE 5

AGE OF 330 COLLEGE DEANS IN RELATION TO TYPES OF STUDENT BODY AND CONTROL

Age	TYPE OF STUDENT BODY			CONTROL			Total
	Men's Colleges	Women's Colleges	Coed. Colleges	Public	Private	Denom.	
20–29	0	1	2	0	0	3	3
30–39	10	6	33	5	6	38	49
40–49	23	21	68	18	24	70	112
50–59	10	18	72	26	22	52	100
60–69	10	10	38	11	14	33	58
70–79	1	0	6	0	4	3	7
80–89	0	0	1	0	0	1	1
Total	54	56	220	60	70	200	330
Median age	46	50	50	52	56	48	50

Table 5 discloses that denominational colleges are more prone to select their deans from the lower age levels than are either the publicly or the privately controlled institutions.

TABLE 6

AGE OF 330 COLLEGE DEANS IN RELATION TO SIZE OF INSTITUTION

Age	SIZE OF INSTITUTION									Total
	250 or Less	250– 500	500– 750	750– 1,000	1,000– 1,500	1,500– 2,000	2,000– 5,000	5,000– 10,000	10,000 and Over	
20–29 ...	1	0	1	1	0	0	0	0	0	3
30–39 ...	10	17	11	3	4	2	1	0	1	49
40–49 ...	20	29	25	12	8	8	7	2	1	112
50–59 ...	8	31	16	7	13	8	14	2	1	100
60–69 ...	8	16	13	7	4	2	5	3	0	58
70–79 ...	0	4	2	1	0	0	0	0	0	7
80–89 ...	0	1	0	0	0	0	0	0	0	1
Total ...	47	98	68	31	29	20	27	7	3	330
Median age ...	44	51	48	49	51	50	53	56	49	50

TABLE 7

AGE OF 330 COLLEGE DEANS IN RELATION TO GEOGRAPHICAL SECTION

Age	GEOGRAPHICAL SECTION									Tota
	New Eng- land	Mid. Atlan- tic	E. No. Cen- tral	W. No. Cen- tral	S. At- lantic	E. So. Cen- tral	W. So. Cen- tral	Moun- tain	Paci- fic	
20–29 ...	0	0	0	1	2	0	0	0	0	3
30–39 ...	2	8	3	8	10	8	6	1	3	49
40–49 ...	10	18	20	13	19	12	9	6	5	112
50–59 ...	8	17	16	18	16	4	9	3	9	100
60–69 ...	2	16	14	6	9	4	3	1	3	58
70–79 ...	1	0	3	1	1	0	0	0	1	7
80–89 ...	0	0	0	1	0	0	0	0	0	1
Total ...	23	59	56	48	57	28	27	11	21	330
Median age ...	49	52	51	51	49	44	48	47	53	50

Tables 6 and 7 reveal the ages of 330 college deans in relation to size of institution and geographical location.

Twenty-eight denominational affiliations were represented in this study. The ten denominational groups having the largest number of colleges reporting at the time tabulation began were analyzed by cross-counts. The remaining eighteen denominational controls, analyzed only by straight-counts because of mechanical limitations, were represented in the study as follows:

Denomination	Number of Colleges	Denomination	Number of Colleges
Christian	5	Church of Christ	1
Reformed	4	Church of God	1
United Brethern	4	Cong. and Episcopal	1
African M. E.	3	Free Methodist	1
Evangelical	3	Latter Day Saints	1
United Presbyterian	3	M. E. and Presbyterian	1
Mennonite	2	Moravian	1
United Lutheran	2	Seventh Day Adventists	1
Christian Reformed	1	Seventh Day Baptists	1

Table 8 presents data concerning the ages of 164 deans in ten denominational college groups.

TABLE 8

AGE OF 164 COLLEGE DEANS IN RELATION TO TEN DENOMINATIONAL GROUPS

Age	DENOMINATIONAL GROUPS										Total
	R. C.	Presb.	M. E.	Bapt.	Luth.	M. E. So.	Fr.	Breth.	Disc.	Cong.	
20–29	0	1	1	0	1	0	0	0	0	0	3
30–39	9	7	5	4	0	3	1	1	1	1	32
40–49	20	7	9	9	2	3	1	3	1	0	55
50–59	10	8	4	4	8	4	3	1	3	1	46
60–69	3	4	5	4	2	3	1	1	0	2	25
70–79	0	0	1	1	0	0	0	0	0	0	2
80–89	0	1	0	0	0	0	0	0	0	0	1
Total	42	28	25	22	13	13	6	6	5	4	164
Median age	45	49	45	49	52	51	51	49	54	60	49

For the various denominational groups, the percentage of deans under 50 years of age and the percentage of deans 60 years and over follow:

Denomination	Per Cent under 50 Years of Age	Per Cent 60 Years of Age and Over
Roman Catholic	69.0%	7.1%
Presbyterian	53.5	17.8
Methodist Episcopal	60.0	24.0
Baptist	59.0	22.7
Lutheran	23.0	15.3
M. E. South	46.1	23.0
Friends	33.3	16.7
Brethern	66.7	16.7
Disciples	40.0	0.0
Congregational	25.0	50.0

WOMEN DEANS IN LIBERAL ARTS COLLEGES

Of the 330 deans reporting in this study, 47 (14.2%) are women. Of these, 44 (93.6%) are in women's colleges and the remaining 3 (6.4%) are in coeducational institutions. As to control, 2 (4.3%) women deans are in public, 20 (42.5%) in private, and 25 (53.2%) in denominational colleges. Of the latter, 17 (68%) are in Roman Catholic, 4 (16%) in Baptist, 2 (8%) in Presbyterian, 1 (4%) in Methodist Episcopal, and 1 (4%) in Reformed colleges. No women deans appear in the Negro colleges reporting.

Women deans are more frequently found in colleges of smaller enrollments. Thirty-seven (78.7%) are in institutions of 750 or less enrollment. No institutions of 5,000 or more enrollment reported women deans. Geographically, they are distributed throughout the United States, with the heaviest percentages in the Middle Atlantic, East North Central, South Atlantic, and New England groups.

DEANS OF NEGRO COLLEGES

All deans of Negro colleges reporting are men. Two Negro colleges are public, 2 private, 1 national and private, and 14 denominational. Of the denominational, 5 are Methodist Episcopal, 2 Baptist, 1 Presbyterian, 1 M. E. South, 1 Congregational, 1 United Presbyterian, and 3 African M. E. All are 750 or less in enrollment, as follows: 250 or less—1, 250-500—12, 500-750—6. Two are men's colleges and 17 are coeducational. Geographically, they are located in five sections, namely, Middle Atlantic—1 (5.3%), East North Central—1 (5.3%), South Atlantic—9 (47.4%), East South Central—4 (21%), West South Central— 4 (21%).

ACADEMIC DEGREES OF DEANS

Academically the dean stands high among his colleagues. Of 330 deans reporting, all but 4 have a Bachelor's degree. Two of these four hold Doctor's degrees and a third has had many years of college training. All four have training readily equivalent to that usually represented by the Bachelor's degree. (Table 9.)

Two hundred thirty-nine (72.4%) have Master's degrees and 161 (48.8%) have Doctor's degrees. An interesting comparison

TABLE 9

ACADEMIC DEGREES OF DEANS IN 330 LIBERAL ARTS COLLEGES

Bachelor's Degree	No. of Deans	Master's Degree	No. of Deans	Doctor's Degree	No. of Deans
A.B.	268	A.M.	214	Ph.D.	152
B.S.	34	M.S.	20	Ed.D.	2
Ph.B.	15	Ed.M.	4	J.D.	2
C.E.	4	M.R.E.	1	D.D.	1
Litt.B.	2			S.T.D.	1
B.L.	1			Ped.D.	1
A.A.	1			Litt.D	1
S.T.B.	1			Docteur de l'université	1
Total.......	326		239		161
Per cent of group	98.8%		72.4%		48.8%

may here be made with Toothman's study of 286 deans of liberal arts colleges, of whom 100% held Bachelor's degrees, 92.6% Master's degrees, and 47.2% Doctor's degrees.[3]

In a study of 95 public junior colleges scattered throughout the United States Green found 100% of the deans holding the Bachelor's degree, 75.2% the Master's degree, and 7.2% the Doctor's degree.[4]

Jones's study of 263 deans of women in colleges and universities throughout the United States reported 90.5% holding the Bachelor's degree, 57.4% the Master's degree, and 15.2% the Doctor's degree.[5]

Sturtevant and Strang's study of deans of women in 64 public, state-supported normal schools and 114 public, state-supported teachers colleges reported academic degrees as follows: Normal schools—78.8% holding Bachelor's degrees, 33.3% the Master's degree, 0.0% the Doctor's degree; Teachers Colleges—89% holding Bachelor's degrees, 44% the Master's degree, 0.0% the Doctor's degree.[6]

The U. S. Survey of Land-Grant Colleges and Universities found the degrees held by staffs of all land-grant colleges to be as

[3] Toothman, H. F., The Academic Dean of the Liberal Arts College, p. 109.

[4] Green, Rhue E., "Administrative Dean of the Public Junior College," School Executives Magazine, Vol. 49, p. 122, November 1929.

[5] Jones, Jane Louise, A Personnel Study of Women Deans in Colleges and Universities, p. 18.

[6] Sturtevant, Sarah M. and Strang, Ruth, A Personnel Study of Deans of Women in Teachers Colleges and Normal Schools, p. 17.

follows: Bachelor's degree—96.4%, Master's degree—58.6%, Doctor's degree—18.19%.[7]

In a study of the staffs of 13 denominational colleges in Minnesota, Kelly found 89% holding the Bachelor's degree, 62.8% the Master's degree, and 19.19% the Doctor's degree.[8]

TABLE 10

SUMMARY OF COMPARATIVE DATA ON ACADEMIC DEGREES

	Per Cent with Bachelor's Degree	Per Cent with Master's Degree	Per Cent with Doctor's Degree
Deans of 95 public junior colleges (Green)	100. %	75.2%	7.2%
Deans of women in 263 colleges and universities (Jones)	90.5	57.4	15.2
Deans of women in 64 normal schools (Sturtevant and Strang)	78.8	33.3	0.0
Deans of women in 114 teachers colleges (Sturtevant and Strang)	89.0	44.0	0.0
Staffs of 13 denominational colleges in Minnesota (Kelly)	89.0	62.8	19.2
Staffs of land-grant colleges and universities (U. S. Survey)	96.4	58.6	18.2
Deans of 286 liberal arts colleges (Toothman)	100.	92.6	47.2
Deans of 330 liberal arts colleges (This Study)	98.8	72.4	48.8

Table 10 reveals that the deans of liberal arts colleges as a group exceed in academic preparation (earned degrees) all other groups on which comparative data are here assembled, particularly in the number of Doctor's degrees.

The institutions granting the deans of the group reporting in this study 161 Doctor's degrees appear in Table 11.

HONORARY DEGREES OF DEANS

Eighty-seven deans (26.3%) of this group hold honorary degrees. Two deans have been the recipient of this honor from three different institutions. Five other deans have been honored by two different institutions. The honorary degrees granted and the number of recipients are shown in Table 12.

[7] U. S. Office of Education, *op. cit.*, p. 587.

[8] Kelly, Robert L., "The Minnesota Colleges, Their Contribution to Society," *Association of American Colleges Bulletin*, Vol. 14, p. 272, May 1928.

TABLE 11

INSTITUTIONS GRANTING THE DOCTOR'S DEGREE TO 161 COLLEGE DEANS

Name of Institution	Ph.D. Degree	Other Doctor's Degree
University of Chicago	19	1 (J.D.)
Columbia University	18	
Johns Hopkins University	10	
Yale University	9	
University of Pennsylvania	7	
Harvard University	6	1 (Ed.D.)
Princeton University	6	
Fordham University	5	
New York University	4	1 (J.D.)
University of Wisconsin	4	
Bryn Mawr College	3	
Catholic University of America	2	1 (S.T.D.)
Cornell University	3	
Northwestern University	3	
University of Heidelberg	3	
University of Iowa	3	
University of Kansas	3	
University of Leipsic	3	
University of Minnesota	3	
University of Virginia	3	
Boston University	2	
Indiana University	2	
Stanford University	2	
University of California	1	1 (Ed.D.)
University of Göttingen	2	
University of Kentucky	2	
University of Michigan	2	
University of Missouri	2	
Brown University	1	
California Institute of Technology	1	
Central University	1	
De Paul University	1	
George Peabody College for Teachers ..	1	
Gregorian University (Rome)	1	
Laval University (Quebec)		1 (S.T.D.)
Lehigh University	1	
Loyola University (Chicago)	1	
Marquette University	1	
Mount Union College		1 (Ped.D.)
Ohio State University	1	
St. Louis University		1 (D.D.)
University of Berlin		1 (Litt.D.)
University of Berne	1	
University of Cincinnati	1	
University of Fribourg (Switzerland) ..	1	
University of Halle	1	
University of Louvain	1	
University of Paris		1 (Docteur de l'université)
University of Pittsburgh	1	
University of Southern California	1	
University of Wurzburg	1	
Vanderbilt University	1	

TABLE 12

HONORARY DEGREES GRANTED TO 87 COLLEGE DEANS

Degree	Number Received	Degree	Number Received
LL.D.	34	S.T.D.	1
Litt.D.	15	D.Th.	1
Sc.D.	13	Pd.D.	1
D.D.	9	Master of Humanities...	1
A.M.	7	Officier d'Académie	1
L.H.D.	6	Chevalier de la Légion	
D.S.S.	2	d'honneur	1
Ph.D.	2		—
M.Pd.	2	Total	96

STUDY IN FOREIGN INSTITUTIONS

Forty-five colleges and universities in foreign lands have enrolled 92 students in all from this group of 330 deans, a number of whom have studied in two or more foreign institutions. The number of deans attending each of these institutions and the number and kinds of degrees awarded them by these institutions are shown in Table 13.

TRAVEL IN FOREIGN LANDS

A large number of this group of deans have traveled in foreign lands. The number who have enjoyed foreign travel and the lands visited by them are shown in Table 14. The table indicates that deans are more prone to travel in European countries than in near-by foreign lands, such as Canada, Mexico, and the South American countries.

PREVIOUS SUBJECT-MATTER FIELDS OF DEANS

The assumption is frequently made that a very large per cent of the deans of liberal arts colleges have come from certain subject-matter fields in which student interest has seemed to wane in recent years. Data tabulated in this study do not confirm this assumption. The data are presented in full in Table 15.

The data presented in Table 15 show that if small classes and light teaching loads have in the past been influential factors in the selection of deans, they are now diminishing forces in such appointments.

TABLE 13

FOREIGN INSTITUTIONS ATTENDED BY AND DEGREES AWARDED TO DEANS
OF 330 AMERICAN COLLEGES

Name of Institution	No. of Deans Attending	No. of Degrees	Title
University of Berlin	11	1	Litt.D.
Oxford University	7		
Cambridge University	5		
University of Bonn	5		
University of Heidelberg	5	3	Ph.D.
American Academy (Rome)	3		
Am. School for Classical Studies (Rome)	3		
University of Fribourg	3	1	Ph.D.
University of Göttingen	3	2	Ph.D.
University of Leipsic	3	1-3	A.M.-Ph.D.
University of Louvain	3	1	Ph.D.
Centro de Estudios (Madrid)	2		
University of Berne	2	1	Ph.D.
University of Edinburgh	2		
University of Jena	2		
University of Marburg	2		
University of Munich	2		
University of Paris	2	1	Docteur de
University of Sorbonne	2		l'université
American Academy (Athens)	1		
Christian University (China)	1		
Collegio de San Anselm's (Rome)	1		
Gregorian University (Rome)	1	1	Ph.D.
Ignatius College (Holland)	1		
Laval University (Quebec)	1	1	S.T.D.
London School of Economics and Research	1		
St. Augustine's College (Belgium)	1		
St. John Bernhard College (Belgium)	1		
Technical Institute (Dresden)	1		
Union Theol. Sem., Foochow Col. (China)	1		
University of Aberdeen	1	1	M.A.
University of Florence	1		
University of Geneva	1		
University of Grenoble	1		
University of Halle	1	1	Ph.D.
University of Perugia	1		
University of Propaganda (Rome)	1		
University of Salamanca	1		
University of Strasburg	1		
University of Vienna	1		
University of Wurzburg	1	1	Ph.D.
Upsala University (Sweden)	1		
Zurich Polytechnic Institute	1		
Zurich University	1		
Total	92	19	

TABLE 14

Foreign Lands Visited by Deans of 330 American Colleges

Lands Visited	No. of Deans	Lands Visited	No. of Deans
European Countries	136	Palestine	3
Canada	20	Egypt	3
Far East	16	Cuba	2
Mediterranean Countries	11	South America	2
Hawaii	9	Around the World	2
Philippine Islands	6	Alaska	2
Mexico	5	Newfoundland	1
Africa	3	Caribbean Countries	1
Near East	3	Central America	1

TABLE 15

Previous Subject-Matter Teaching Fields of Deans of 330 Colleges

Previous Subject-Matter Teaching Field	No. of Deans	Total	Per Cent
Education, Philosophy and Psychology—			
Department of Education	35		
Philosophy	15		
Psychology	4		
Philosophy and Psychology	4	58	17.6%
Science—			
Chemistry	17		
Biology	11		
Physics	10		
Natural Sciences	9		
Geology	3		
Zoology	2		
Agriculture	2	54	16.3
Social Studies—			
History	31		
Economics	9		
Political Science	8		
Sociology	3	51	15.5
Literary Studies—			
English	42		
Public Speaking	2	44	13.3
Administration	30	30	9.1
Ancient Languages—			
Latin and Greek	23	23	7.0
Mathematics	15	15	4.5
Religion and Biblical Literature	13	13	4.0
Modern Languages	10	10	3.0
Civil Engineering	2	2	0.6
Research	2	2	0.6
Extension Work	1	1	0.3
Omitted	27	27	8.2

The deans of the 330 liberal arts colleges included in this study have served in a variety of fields before assuming their present deanship. Quite the largest number (82.4%) have, at one time or another, been college instructors. Twenty-seven (8.2%) have been presidents or acting-presidents of institutions. Fifty-nine (18%) have had experience in some type of deanship. Thirty-three (10%) have been either superintendent or assistant-superintendent of state, county, or city schools. Seventy-six (23%) have served either as principal or as assistant-principal of elementary or high schools.

Table 16 shows the educational offices in which the 330 deans participating in this study have previously served, together with the number of deans serving in each type of office.

From Table 16 it is seen that 240 educational offices previously held by these deans have been of the administrative type. A number of deans served in two or more types of administrative office. The actual number who have had previous administrative experience is 160 (48.4%). More than half of the deans in this group had had no administrative experience previous to their present appointment.

TENURE, AND ADMINISTRATIVE AND EDUCATIONAL EXPERIENCE

The criticism is frequently made that deans tend to be appointed, in many colleges and universities, from those faculty members long associated with the institution. Table 17 shows that of the 330 deans included in this study, 4 (1.2%) had been associated with the institution for 30 years or more before appointment to the deanship, 21 (6.3%) for 20 years or more, and 82 (24.8%) for 10 years or more.

On the other hand, 120 (36.3%) were entirely new in the institution, 81 (24.5%) had been with it 5 years or less, and 62 more (18.7%) had served from 6 to 10 years. In other words, 263 deans (79.6%) were appointed to the office after having served not more than 10 years in the institution, 201 deans (60.9%) after not more than 5 years, and 120 deans (36.3%) had never before served on the same staff.

These data would seem to disclaim, therefore, any marked tendency on the part of colleges and universities to select their deans

TABLE 16

EDUCATIONAL OFFICES PREVIOUSLY HELD BY 330 COLLEGE DEANS

Title of Office (On college level)	No. of Deans	Title of Office (On other levels)	No. of Deans
Professor	272	High School Instructor	95
Head of Department	39	Principal of High School	59
College Dean	38	Elementary Teacher	31
President	23	City Superintendent	26
Registrar	19	Principal of Ele. School	11
Vice-President	11	Asst.-Principal, High School	6
Dean of Men	6	County Superintendent	3
Assistant-Dean	5	State Superintendent	2
Acting-President	4	Asst.-State Superintendent	1
Secretary of Faculty	3	Asst.-City Superintendent	1
Dean of Women	2	Sec. of State Bd. of Examiners	1
Dean of Discipline	2		
Treasurer	2		
Librarian	2		
Acting Dean	1		
Class Dean	1		
Assistant to President	1		
Dean of Students	1		
Director of Studies	1		
Director of School	1		
Prefect of Junior College	1		
Secretary of College	1		
Field Secretary	1		
Business Manager	1		
Recorder	1		
Sec. of Bd. of Admissions	1		
Head of Residence Hall	1		
Director of Ed. Research	1		
Research Worker	1		

from staff members of long service in the institution. They would strongly indicate, on the contrary, that there is a distinct tendency to select deans from outside the institution or from those groups of staff members who have been with the college not more than 5 or 10 years. The median is 4.06 years. It safely can be assumed, in the light of these data, that while the practice of conferring the deanship as a recognition of service to the institution covering many years is still discernible, the instances are becoming more and more rare. It has, in fact, ceased to be the practice; it is now, rather, the exception.

The fact that 170 deans (51.5%) had had no administrative experience prior to appointment to their present deanship is a

TABLE 17

PREVIOUS TENURE IN INSTITUTION, PREVIOUS ADMINISTRATIVE EXPERIENCE, TOTAL EDUCATIONAL EXPERIENCE, AND TENURE IN PRESENT DEANSHIP OF 330 COLLEGE DEANS

Years	In Institution before Appointed Dean	Previous Administrative Experience	Total Educational Experience	Present Tenure
0	120	170		12
1	10	18		22
2	24	20		20
3	10	15	1	29
4	16	14	1	25
5	21	17	1	22
6	17	11	9	12
7	9	6	5	12
8	12	6	4	22
9	9	10	12	13
10	15	6	7	23
11	6	5	10	13
12	9	4	13	10
13	6	2	9	17
14	3	4	7	9
15	5	4	3	12
16	6	6	17	10
17	4	1	7	4
18	4	1	12	10
19	3	2	11	3
20	9	2	10	6
21	2	4	9	5
22	2		14	5
23			11	1
24	3		9	4
25			9	1
26		1	10	3
27			8	1
28			10	
29	1		16	
30	1		13	
31	1		8	1
32	2		7	1
33		1	8	
34			5	2
35			5	
36			12	
37			5	
38			3	
39			4	
40			4	
41			4	
42			2	
43			2	
44			3	
45			2	
46			1	
47			1	
48			1	
49			1	
50			1	
51			1	
52			2	
Median	4.06	0	23.27	8.5

matter for serious consideration.   Toothman found that 46.71% of the deans in 286 liberal arts colleges had had no previous administrative experience.[9]

Other studies have revealed a lack of training for the office through professional courses pursued in universities.   Toothman found only 48 deans (16.78%) out of 286 who had taken such courses in college or university.[10]

Jones found that only 19.6% of deans of women in colleges and universities had pursued professional courses.[11]

Sturtevant and Strang reported that 48.5% of deans of women in normal schools and teachers colleges had taken some professional courses.[12]

Deficiencies here revealed in both previous administrative experience and professional training strongly indicate a less than satisfactory preparation for the office in at least 50% of the cases. The lack of direct preparation through professional courses may be accounted for partly, with these groups of deans, by the fact that courses preparing directly for the deanship only recently came into the curricula of universities.   Teachers College, Columbia University, the University of Chicago, the George Peabody College for Teachers, and other institutions are now offering courses of this nature, which innovation should tend greatly to improve the situation.

While courses involving specific techniques of the deanship doubtless have distinct values for those preparing for this office, no such high degree of standardization as to make them requisite is here advocated.   Broad general and fundamental study of the problems of higher education as a whole, rather than minute, specific techniques used therein, should have major emphasis. Adequate training of this type, both theoretical and practical, should increase the efficiency of the deans and enhance the educational importance of the office.   This improvement may confidently be anticipated as adequate professional preparation becomes more and more an essential requirement for the deanship.

In point of educational experience, which includes experience in the present position, the deans are a mature group.   No deans in this study have been in educational work less than three years,

[9] Toothman, *op. cit.*, p. 114.
[10] *Ibid.*, p. 112.
[11] Jones, *op. cit.*, p. 21.
[12] Sturtevant and Strang, *op. cit.*, p. 19.

only three less than six years, and only thirty-three less than ten years.

In the matter of tenure in their present position, the record of these 330 deans is noteworthy. Twelve of them had just assumed the office at the beginning of the 1933-34 academic year. Since this study covers the years previous to 1933-34, these twelve deans show no tenure in the deanship. Including them in the table, however, the range is 34 years and the median 8.5 years. Since these deans are still serving in these positions, the median may not seem a true measure of their tenure. The middle 50%, or interquartile range, which seems a better measure, shows a range of 10 years (3 to 13) and the same median of 8.5 years.

Green found the median tenure for junior college deans to be 4.5 years, with a range of 2.6 to 8.5 years for the middle 50%.[13]

Leonard, Evenden and O'Rear found the median tenure of the typical staff members of fourteen Lutheran colleges to be 4 years.[14]

The State Survey Commission for higher education in Missouri found the median tenure for the staff members of five state teachers colleges in Missouri to be 6 years and stated:

These figures do not vary widely from comparable figures obtained from other teacher training institutions.[15]

The same commission reported 6 years as the median tenure for staff members at the University of Missouri, 8 years at the School of Mines at Rolla, Missouri, and 3 years at Lincoln University.[16]

The Educational Survey Commission of the State of Florida found the median tenure for staff members at the University of Florida and the Florida State College for Women combined to be about 3⅓ years.[17]

Reeves reported the median tenure of staff members of all ranks combined at the University of Chicago to be 6.1 years.[18]

The median tenure of the 330 deans participating in this study is, therefore, 4 years greater than the median tenure of junior

[13] Green, op. cit., p. 123.

[14] Leonard, R. J., Evenden, E. S., O'Rear, F. B., and Others, Survey of Higher Education for the United Lutheran Church in America, Vol. 1, p. 281.

[15] The State Survey Commission, Publicly Supported Higher Education in the State of Missouri, November, 1929, p. 362.

[16] Ibid., pp. 93, 469.

[17] Educational Survey Commission of the State of Florida, Official Report of the Educational Survey Commission of the State of Florida, April 2, 1929, p. 528.

[18] Reeves, F. W. and Others, The University Faculty, The University of Chicago Survey, 1933, Vol. 3, p. 61.

college deans and exceeds the median tenure of the typical college staff member as revealed by comparable data of available studies. Considering the great diversity of these 330 institutions as to type, size, control, age and geographical location, a median tenure of 8.5 years is indeed complimentary to the present incumbents of the office and convincing testimony to the value and stability of the college deanship.

SUMMARY

This chapter has presented personal and professional background data of 330 deans in liberal arts colleges in the United States. These data reveal that the deans as a group are mature individuals; that the great majority of deanships are held by men; that the dean ranks high, academically, among his colleagues; that one-fourth of the deans in this group have been awarded honorary degrees by colleges and universities; that the study and travel of deans in foreign lands have been varied and extensive; that the subject-matter fields of Education, Philosophy and Psychology, of Science, of Social Studies, and of English yield by far the largest number of deans, with relatively small percentages coming from the fields of the Ancient Languages, Mathematics, and Religion; that the tenure record is commendable.

The educational experience of these deans prior to their appointment to the deanship has included a wide variety of fields. More than four-fifths of them have been college instructors. Less than half of them had had administrative experience previously and a comparatively small percentage had pursued professional courses in universities preparing directly for the deanship.

The data further indicate that there is no longer any marked tendency to confer the office merely as recognition of long service to the institution. A very large number of deans are selected from outside the institution or from groups of staff members who have served the college not more than five or ten years.

CHAPTER V

Validity and Reliability of Instruments

THREE types of materials were used in this study: (1) the historical questionnaire, (2) the "Test on Controversial Issues," and (3) the instrument.

The first of these—the historical questionnaire—primarily sought professional information, with a minimum of merely personal data. A thorough study of the responses indicates that this information was freely and willingly supplied and that the questionnaire served its purpose to an adequate extent.

As to the validity and reliability of the "Test on Controversial Issues," Dr. Cottrell's own discussion of these aspects in his article published in the *Teachers College Record* for May, 1933, is the best available justification.[1] Satisfactory reliability has been achieved for the Professional-Centered, Experience-Centered, and Classroom Teaching-Centered traits. Research is now in progress to find means of increasing the reliability for the tests of the Classic-Centered, Administration-Centered and Research-Centered traits.

The third of the materials—the instrument—was constructed and used initially in this study. It is therefore relevant to inquire what it really measures and how reliable this measurement is.

VALIDITY OF THE INSTRUMENT

While the instrument is not actually a true-false test, since there are no "right" nor "wrong" answers, it essentially involves that technique. It should, therefore, satisfy the major criteria established and generally accepted for the true-false type of instrument. These criteria are as follows:

1. The technique must be suitable to the problem studied.

2. The language of the instrument must be clear, concise, readily understood, and non-ambiguous.

---

[1] Cottrell, Donald Peery, "The Measurement of Conflicting Viewpoints in Higher Education," *Teachers College Record*, Vol. XXXIV, pp. 635-54, May 1933.

3. Thorough and painstaking revision must be made of the instrument and adequate refinement achieved before it is used in the investigation.

4. The multiple-choice statements must be sufficiently comprehensive and inclusive in content and scope to cover adequately the field explored.

In regard to the first criterion, the purpose of the study was to discover the opinions, preferences, judgments, and controlling ideas of the individuals responding. For that purpose the multiple-choice type of instrument seems highly suitable. A criticism may be offered that not in every case were satisfactory alternatives supplied and that, therefore, the responding individual was not given opportunity adequately to express himself. The pertinence of this criticism is readily admitted. The defense offered is that the statements were framed, criticized, and revised with meticulous care, that where the issue was forced it was so designed, and that choice by the individual of one alternative meant discrimination only in respect to the specific alternatives offered for that statement.

To effect satisfaction of the second criterion, the coöperative effort of a large number of individuals—many expert in this field —was secured. Criticism of the language in which statements were worded was particularly sought and generously given by professors, deans, graduate students, and laymen. It is worthy to be noted that when the instrument was submitted in its final form in the investigation, there was practically no criticism as to clarity or meaning of statement by any of the 330 deans responding.

While ambiguity of language may be effectively dealt with in such an instrument, ambiguity of alternatives to statements presents a real difficulty. Ambiguity of this type does exist in some instances in this instrument. However, alternatives were not designed to be mutually exclusive in the cases of all item choices. As explained in a preceding paragraph, and in the instructions for marking, the individual was to circle the letter in front of the alternative which most nearly agreed with his way of thinking. It was, therefore, expected that, in some instances, the individual marking the instrument would be in some agreement with more than one alternative to certain of the statements. He might not be in complete agreement with any one of them. But his marking would indicate his preference for one over the others, and would express the point of his emphasis. To effect this purpose the issue was therefore forced in certain instances, but the individual's choice of one alternative expressed his discrimination only as to the specific alternatives offered by the statement. This made it possible to determine the opinion of the group on certain controversial issues. Alternatives thus chosen have been preserved in their original context in all the discussion throughout this study.

As to the third criterion, the process of revision has already been described in Chapter II. Preliminary try-outs were made with various groups—deans, graduate students in higher education, and members of staffs of various colleges. They were asked to suggest additional statements, additional alternatives, simplifications of language, etc., and in most instances their written criticisms were followed by personal interviews which yielded valuable information for revision purposes. The process of revision covered the greater part of one year and was participated in by a large number of individuals acquainted with the field of college administration.

In regard to the final criterion, it was recognized early in the progress of the study that all areas involving college administration could not be covered adequately by one instrument convenient enough in length to secure response from a large number of busy administrators. Not less than 75 nor more than 100 multiple-choice statements seemed the optimum number for such a study. In order to be certain of adequate treatment, the number of areas was therefore restricted to four and the final number of statements to 76. These four areas—(1) purpose of the college, (2) curriculum, (3) improvement of instruction, and (4) student welfare—were deliberately chosen because of their vital connection with the office of dean and their apparently close relation to present college readjustment programs.

The literature of these four fields was then explored for controversial issues related to the philosophy of administration, and this was supplemented by interviews with prominent educators. During the revision process additional suggestions were invited from deans, college professors, and students of education in general. In these varied ways statements were at length secured sufficiently comprehensive in scope and content to cover adequately the four fields of exploration.

All statements referring to one area were grouped consecutively under that heading in what seemed a logical arrangement. The purpose of each item choice was clearly to divide opinion, but in the scoring the classification of the individual was made upon his total response to the instrument and never upon a single item choice in a particular field nor upon the total item choices within a single area.

Supporting the claim for validity is the fact that an inspection of scores of individuals shows a high consistency of marking throughout the instrument. Such an inspection also reveals the fact that the instrument did divide opinion between the "right" and the "left" in regard to philosophy of administration. Validity was further substantiated by the individual marking of the graphic self-rating scales. While there were occasional glaring inconsistencies between an individual's score and his own mark on the self-rating scale, in general there was a satisfactory degree of association. This should be expected, however, since the significance of the responses was basically determined by the aggregate self-rating scale marks, but it measurably justified the correctness of the mathematical processes employed.

To further gauge the validity of the instrument, individual scores were checked against the individual's own opinion of his position, as revealed in conference, and against the opinion of close friends intimately acquainted with his positions on various issues. In a number of cases it was possible to scrutinize the published writings of individuals and check their deliberately-expressed positions against their markings of the instrument. The general consensus, after the use of all these methods, was that the instrument did reveal the views of the various individuals so checked to a very significant degree.

On the instruments returned by the 330 deans many written comments were made that indicated both ready comprehension of meaning and conscientious marking. There was no indication from such comments that the language was vague nor its purport misunderstood. Erasures, altered markings, question marks, and sometimes lengthy notations testified to the interest and effort of the marker. Candid and frank expressions were further encouraged by the fact that no name appeared upon the instrument. Often, however, personal letters expressing interest in the study were returned with the questionnaires, together with a request for a digest of the findings.

RELIABILITY OF THE INSTRUMENT

To determine the reliability of the instrument, two procedures were followed. After an interval of several months the instrument was administered a second time to a group of professors, deans, and graduate students in higher education. The correlation between the scores of these two successive markings was .857 ± .04, which is sufficiently high to indicate a significant reliability for the instrument.

A statistical study was also made of the self-reliability of the instrument by checking one half against the other half. The scores of odds and evens on both the democratic and the autocratic responses from 110 instruments were correlated, and the correlations "stepped up" by the Spearman-Brown formula. The correlations were found to be:

Democratic items .... $r = .6412 ± .04$
With Spearman-Brown formula .... $r = .7813 ± .02$

Autocratic items .... $r = .7054 ± .03$
With Spearman-Brown formula .... $r = .8272 ± .02$

Since a .75 to .80 coefficient is usually regarded as satisfactory for group test purposes,[2] these correlations suggest significant reliability for the instrument used in this study.

By various methods of inspection and checking, the validity of the instrument is evidenced, while statistical treatment confirms conclusions as to its reliability. It therefore may well qualify as an acceptable measure for use in this investigation.

CONSTRUCTION OF THE SCORING KEY

For the purposes of this study, two opposing conceptions of college administration—democratic and autocratic—were selected and defined on the last page of the instrument as follows:

Extreme autocratic administration as here defined is by a board of laymen chosen for life by coöptation, clothed with complete authority, delegating certain powers to a president of their own choosing, the president exercising these powers, with the faculty entirely subordinated and student opinion repressed or disregarded. Extreme democratic administration is understood to be that where all control is in the hands of the faculty and students.

[2] Kelley, Truman L., *Interpretation of Educational Measurements*, p. 210.

Following these definitions was a graphic self-rating scale on which the individual marking the instrument was asked to express his preference for the democratic or autocratic conception of college administration, as specifically defined in the preceding paragraph.

Of the 330 deans returning usable replies, their self-markings on the scale were as follows:

Group	Scale	No.	Per Cent of Group
1. Strongly democratic	(75.1%–100%) (D)	108	33
2. Democratic	(50.1%– 75%) (D)	111	34
3. Neutral	(50.0%)	43	13
4. Autocratic	(50.1%– 75%) (A)	54	16
5. Strongly autocratic	(75.1%–100%) (A)	13	4
Y. Omitted		1	

The replies of the two democratic groups combined were then compared with the replies of the combined autocratic groups on each item choice, after the following procedure:

a. The number of the 219 deans responding to each of the item choices of the instrument who, by their mark on the self-rating scale, registered themselves as more favorable to the democratic viewpoint, was tabulated.

b. The number of the 67 deans responding to each of the item choices of the instrument who, by their mark on the self-rating scale, registered themselves as more favorable to the autocratic viewpoint, was tabulated.

c. These two numbers, in relation to the numbers of both groups who did not respond to the item, were then compared for each item choice separately by means of the Yule fourfold *r*.

d. The item choices that were thus shown to have a sufficiently high coefficient of correlation as to be definitely attractive choices for those who considered themselves democratic were classified as "democratic responses"; likewise, definitely attractive choices for those who considered themselves autocratic were classified as "autocratic responses."

An item choice was regarded as significant when, by the use of the equation $Nr^2 = X^2$, its coefficient of correlation was sufficiently large that X^2 should be at least 3.841 when

$$X^2 = \frac{(ad - bc)^2 \, (N)}{(a + c) \, (b + d) \, (a + b) \, (c + d)}.$$

Such a value for X^2 is so large that it could have occurred by chance not more than 5 times in 100. By computation it was found that the r for each democratic or autocratic item choice must be at least .12 in order to be significant.

An example of the application of the Yule fourfold formula follows:

"Purpose of the College"

3. The purpose of a liberal arts college
   a. Should adapt itself to the present needs of students (78%) (D)

	Responded with item choice	Did not respond with item choice	
Number high on democratic scale	186	33	219
Number high on autocratic scale	40	27	67
	226	60	

$$\frac{(186 \times 27) - (40 \times 33)}{\sqrt{226 \times 60 \times 67 \times 219}} = +.2625.$$

The significant item choices determined in this manner are listed in Table 18, together with the Yule fourfold r for each significant item choice.

This analysis yielded 27 significant "democratic responses" and 33 significant "autocratic responses." While the method was conceded to be extremely rigid, decision was made to stay within its limits. Consequently, only the responses listed in Table 18 were used in the construction of the scoring key.

Fifteen other responses that showed a distinct leaning toward the democratic conception and fifteen other responses that showed a distinct leaning toward the autocratic conception, though not included in the scoring key, are listed in Table 19.

Each of the 330 instruments was scored by means of the scoring key, presented in Table 18. The number of "democratic responses" minus the number of "autocratic responses," or vice versa as the case might be, constituted the final score of the individual. With the exception of a few outstanding cases, the final score corresponded rather closely to the individual's mark of his own preference on the graphic self-rating scale. Though a few

TABLE 18

SIGNIFICANT DEMOCRATIC AND AUTOCRATIC ITEM CHOICES FOR 330 DEANS

Item	Significance	Yule 4-fold r	Item	Significance	Yule 4-fold r
"Purpose of College"			*"Student Welfare"*		
3.a	D*	.26	1.a	D	.18
c	A*	.26	b	A	.18
4.a	A	.19	2.a	A	.17
b	D	.16	d	D	.18
6.a	D	.12	3.b	A	.13
7.b	A	.26	4.a	A	.20
c	D	.27	b	D	.20
12.a	A	.28	5.b	A	.15
c	D	.25	6.c	A	.14
13.b	A	.12	d	D	.14
			10.c	D	.13
"Curriculum"			11.a	D	.15
2.b	D	.12	b	A	.14
c	A	.12	12.a	A	.12
3.a	A	.22	b	D	.12
b	D	.26	c	D	.12
5.a	D	.12	14.a	A	.15
7.c	A	.12	17.a	D	.12
8.c	A	.12	b	A	.14
10.a	D	.12	18.c	A	.23
b	A	.12	21.a	A	.12
11.b	D	.24	22.a	A	.21
c	A	.24	c	D	.18
12.b	A	.23	23.c	A	.15
			24.a	A	.26
"Improvement of Instruction"			c	D	.20
2.b	D	.13			
3.a	A	.20			
b	D	.16			
4.c	A	.13			
10.b	D	.18			
12.c	D	.14			
14.a	A	.19			
c	D	.12			
17.a	A	.13			
b	A	.13			
c	D	.20			
26.c	A	.14			

* "A"—Autocratic.   "D"—Democratic.

TABLE 19

THIRTY ADDITIONAL ITEM CHOICES THAT SHOW DISTINCT LEANINGS

Item	Leaning	Yule r	Item	Leaning	Yule r
"Purpose of College"			*"Improvement of Instruction"*		
3.b	A*	.1053	2.a	A	.1097
5.a	A	.1051	4.b	D	.1095
7.a	A	.0918	10.c	A	.0815
9.c	A	.1102	11.a	A	.1040
13.a	D*	.1113	12.b	A	.1038
			21.b	A	.1109
"Curriculum"			25.a	D	.0998
1.a	A	.0937			
b	D	.095	*"Student Welfare"*		
3.c	A	.1083	2.b	D	.1023
5.b	A	.1005	3.a	D	.1014
6.c	D	.0864	5.a	D	.0930
7.b	D	.0899	10.b	A	.0876
8.a	D	.0874	15.b	A	.0840
12.a	D	.1106	18.b	D	.1106
c	D	.096	19.c	A	.1026
			21.c	D	.1057
			23.a	D	.0889

* "A"—Autocratic.   "D"—Democratic Conception.

individuals marked themselves at one or the other extreme end of the scale, no final score was perfect for either classification.

SUMMARY

This chapter has related how the major criteria for validity of the instrument used in this study were satisfied in its construction. It has presented the methods of statistical treatment whereby the reliability of the instrument was confirmed.

A detailed description has also been given of the process by which the scoring key was constructed, and the scoring key itself was presented in table form.

CHAPTER VI

Analysis and Interpretation of Responses

THE purpose of this chapter is to analyze, by the best available methods, the data gathered in this study and to set forth the more significant items revealed in the responses of the deans to the statements of the instrument which definitely involved, as statistical treatment indicated, the democratic and autocratic conceptions of college administration. It should be stated at the outset that no high degree of objectivity is claimed for the various mathematical processes employed in interpretation. Their shortcomings are promptly acknowledged. But that these processes have, nevertheless, a certain value when used judiciously is the general belief of those who have studied them most intensively.

To discover any significant relationship between kind of philosophy of administration and certain other factors, an analysis was made of democratic and autocratic marks on the self-rating scales as compared with (1) age of deans, (2) sex, (3) type of control of institution, (4) denomination, (5) size of college or university, (6) type of student body, (7) geographical location, and (8) race. The data for these comparisons are presented in Table 20. The figures in the percentage columns represent the per cent of each group that marked themselves "democratic" or "autocratic" on the self-rating scales. The figures in the column marked "significance" represent the quotient obtained by dividing the actual percentage difference by the probable error of the difference. Only quotients indicating significance (4 or more) are reported.

RELATION OF PHILOSOPHY MARK TO OTHER FACTORS

Table 20 reveals that all groups showed a preference for the democratic over the autocratic conception of college administration that was statistically significant, with the exception of these groups: Age—20-29, 70-79; Denomination—Roman Catholic, Lutheran; Size—2000-5000, 5000-10,000; Type of Student Body —men's colleges; Geographical Sections—New England, Pacific.

TABLE 20

DEMOCRATIC AND AUTOCRATIC PERCENTAGES OF GROUPS AS BASED UPON
MARKS OF SELF-RATING SCALES

	Factor	Dem. %	Aut. %	Significance Dem.	Significance Aut.
Age	20–29	67	33		
	30–39	64	22	6.86	
	40–49	64	24	9.82	
	50–59	71	14	14.88	
	60–69	66	21	8.18	
	70–79	57	29		
	80–89	100	0	D*	
	Under 50 years of age	64	24	11.94	
	50 years and over	69	17	16.66	
Sex	Male	67	19	21.81	
	Female	64	27	5.69	
Control	Public	62	18	8.16	
	Private	64	20	8.75	
	Denominational	69	21	16.72	
Denomina-tion	Roman Catholic	38	46		
	Presbyterian	78	14	9.31	
	Methodist Episcopal	76	12	8.87	
	Baptist	82	18	8.18	
	Lutheran	69	23		
	M. E. South	76	15	5.87	
	Friends	83	17	4.52	
	Brethern	100	0	D	
	Disciples	80	0	D	
	Congregational	75	0	D	
	Total Protestant groups	79	14	19.94	
Size	250 or less	63	25	5.98	
	250–500	72	20	12.80	
	500–750	68	18	10.14	
	750–1000	71	16	7.81	
	1000–1500	65	14	6.94	
	1500–2000	65	15	8.91	
	2000–5000	52	29		
	5000–10,000	28	43		
	10,000 and over	100	0	D	
Type of Student Body	Men's Colleges	45	39		
	Women's Colleges	66	27	5.82	
	Coeducational Colleges	72	14	22.65	
Geographical Section	New England	39	44		
	Middle Atlantic	70	16	10.63	
	East North Central	59	19	7.13	
	West North Central	71	15	10.05	
	South Atlantic	70	25	8.00	
	East South Central	71	18	7.01	
	West South Central	78	11	10.00	
	Mountain	90	9	9.63	
	Pacific	52	34		
Race	White	65	30	13.88	
	Negro	79	11	8.57	

* "D" indicates vote was 100% "Democratic."
Note: Per cent of each group voting neutral (50–50) omitted from this table.

Of these latter groups, only the Roman Catholic, 5000-10,000 enrollment and New England groups showed a larger percentage for the autocratic than the democratic philosophy of administration. No group, by this method, showed a significant preference for the autocratic conception.

The Yule fourfold formula, by which the significant democratic and autocratic responses were determined, if applied to the self-rating scale marks of the members of the various groups, would tend to show the relation between each group and the total group of deans in their preference for the democratic or autocratic conception. Its application would yield the following statistically significant classifications:

Democratic—Coeducational Colleges, West South Central groups.
Autocratic—Roman Catholic, Men's Colleges, New England groups.

It would further indicate the following strong tendencies:

Inclined Democratic—Age 50-59, Male, Brethren, Presbyterian, Methodist Episcopal, Disciples, West North Central, Mountain, Negro groups.
Inclined Autocratic—Age 40-49, Female, 2000-5000 and 5000-10,000 enrollment, Women's Colleges, Pacific, White groups.

SATISFACTORY MINIMUM INDEX OF CONSENSUS

To evaluate properly the responses of the group of 330 deans to the various item choices of the instrument it was first necessary to determine a satisfactory minimum index of consensus. To secure a percentage figure large enough to constitute a reliable determination of preference for a given item, the reliable percentage for the responses to the various items of the instrument used in this study was defined as one at least 3σ above 50%. The formula to be used, then, was

$$P(\text{percentage}) - .50 > 3 \sqrt{\frac{P(1-P)}{330}}.$$

Squaring both sides of this inequality, and solving the resulting quadratic equation for P, the reliable percentage was found to be 58.15 for every item of the instrument. This minimum index was considered satisfactory for a group of 330 judges, since the probability that a second jury of 330 similarly qualified judges would reverse the verdict is less than two chances in a thousand. This probability was determined in the following manner:

If we assume that Item Choice A has been rated over Item

Choice B with a 58.15% agreement in a jury of 330 individuals, then the standard deviation of this percent is

$$\sigma = \frac{(.5815)\,(.4185)}{330} = .027$$

The probability that another jury similar to this one would rate B over A is the probability that this percentage of agreement would fall below .50. But .5815 − .50 = .0815, which is three times the standard deviation. On page 5, in Table II of Tables of the Probability Integral, of Pearson's *Tables for Statisticians and Biometricians,* the area under the normal curve up to the ordinate corresponding to $X = 3\ \sigma$ is .9986501 of the entire area under the curve.[1] This leaves only .0013499 of the area beyond this ordinate. Therefore, .0013499 is the probability that a new jury, similarly constituted, would rate B over A. This is less than two chances in a thousand.

ANALYSIS OF RESPONSES

The percentage vote of the total group for each item choice was calculated. Cross-counts were then run on the 54 statements considered most important in this study, and the percentage vote of the various groups for each item of these 54 statements was

TABLE 21

DEMOCRATIC AND AUTOCRATIC ITEM CHOICES THAT RECEIVED A RELIABLE PERCENTAGE VOTE FROM TOTAL GROUP OF 330 DEANS

Area	DEMOCRATIC ITEMS		AUTOCRATIC ITEMS	
	High Reliable Percentage Items (75%–100%)	Reliable Percentage Items (59%–74.9%)	High Reliable Percentage Items (75%–100%)	Reliable Percentage Items (59%–74.9%)
Purpose of College ..	3a(78%) 7c(84%)	4b(68%) 12c(71%)		13b(65%)
Curriculum	5a(75%) 11b(84%)	10a(65%)		
Improvement of Instruction	17c(85%)	2b(62%) 3b(70%)		
Student Welfare	6d(85%) 22c(97%)	1a(69%) 11a(72%) 12b(59%)		4a(59%) 17b(73%)
Total	7	8	0	3

[1] Pearson, Karl, *Tables for Statisticians and Biometricians,* p. 5.

computed. Using the criterion of the reliable percentage, 43 items were found to be in this classification. As explained in the preceding chapter (pages 51 ff.), 27 significant democratic and 33 significant autocratic responses were determined by the Yule four-fold formula. Table 21 shows the democratic and autocratic responses, for each area, that received a reliable percentage vote from the total group of 330 deans.

Table 21 shows that of the significant items that obtained reliable percentage votes, 83% were democratic and 17% autocratic responses. These data, therefore, also indicate that the 330 deans reporting in this study are, as a group, definitely inclined toward the democratic conception of college administration.

ANALYSIS OF GROUP VOTES ON ITEMS OF TABLE 21

An analysis of group votes on the 18 significant responses that secured a reliable percentage support reveals certain important facts and is therefore given in detail.

"Purpose of the College"

3. The purpose of a liberal arts college
   a. should adapt itself to the present needs of students (78%) (D)
   b. should change only if the supporting constituency changes (6%)
   c. should generally remain permanent during the life of the institution (12%) (A)

The high percentage vote for Item a distinctly indicates the trend among administrators to adapt the liberal arts college to the present needs of its students. All geographical sections favored this response, the range being from 62% (Pacific group) to 89% (East South Central group). The coeducational college group, in comparison with both the men's college and women's college groups, showed a percentage difference statistically significant in favor of the democratic response. The publicly-controlled group gave an 85% vote to this item; the private and denominational groups gave it a 77% vote. The Presbyterian, Methodist Episcopal, Baptist and Friends groups, and all nine Protestant groups combined, favored the democratic response, as compared with the Roman Catholic preference for this item, by a statistically significant percentage difference.

4. Higher education will best be developed and improved by
   a. continuing the present competitive processes among colleges (23%)
   (A)

    b. eliminating these competitive processes and establishing voluntary cooperative agencies (68%) (D)

On this statement no reliable percentage difference appeared as to race, age, or type of control, though the deans of Negro colleges supported Item *b* by a higher percentage (84%) than did the deans of the White college group (67%).

The coeducational group definitely preferred the democratic response more strongly than the men's college group. Deans of Protestant colleges as a whole, and of Presbyterian and Methodist Episcopal groups in particular, voted much more decisively for this item than did the Roman Catholic group. Among geographical sections, the New England group alone failed to register a preference for the democratic response. A percentage difference of definite reliability appeared on this item between the New England group and the South Atlantic, East South Central, and West South Central groups.

7. The purpose of a college can best be realized by placing the responsibility for internal administration
    a. entirely in the hands of the president and board of trustees (2%)
    b. entirely in the hands of the president, deans and executive officers (12%) (A)
    c. in the hands of the administrators and faculty in cooperation (84%) (D)
    d. in the hands of the faculty alone (1%)

This statement essentially involves the philosophy of college administration. As indicated above, the democratic response drew a very high reliable percentage, the autocratic response drew a low minority vote, and the extremes of the two positions received negligible support.

In general, all groups favored Item *c*, some more emphatically than others. Those in the latter classification are: Age—50 years and older; Control—private; Denomination—Presbyterian, Friends, Brethern; Size—10,000 and over; Type of Student Body —women's college, coeducational; Geographical Sections—West North Central, New England, Mountain; Race—White.

Among the denominations, the Presbyterian, Friends and Brethern groups showed a significant preference for the democratic response over the Roman Catholic group. Likewise, the Presbyterian group showed a significant preference for the democratic response over the Methodist Episcopal group.

12. The liberal arts college of the future
    a. should continue to conserve and transmit classical knowledge (18%) (A)
    b. should become more professional and vocational in character (5%)
    c. should endeavor to foster experiences for the rounded development of its students (71%) (D)

Analyses as to age and sex show no significant differences. All denominational groups show a reliable percentage difference in their preferences for the democratic response over both of the other responses except the Roman Catholic, which shows a reliable percentage difference in favor of the autocratic over the democratic item. The latter's vote, outstandingly at variance with the votes of all other denominational groups, was as follows: a— 57%, b—5%, c—33%. When compared with preferences of the other denominational groups, the preference of the Roman Catholic group for the autocratic response shows a reliable percentage difference in all cases except the Lutheran group. Four groups— Methodist Episcopal, Friends, Brethern, and Disciples—cast no vote for this response.

No significant differences appeared among the groups as to size, type of student body, or geographical section. The Negro college group, in their preference for the democratic response, showed a reliable percentage difference when compared with the similar preference of the White college group.

13. The primary effect of a national educational college entrance policy would be to
    a. eliminate wasteful competition and overlapping (30%)
    b. give too much power to a central authority, thus tending to stereotype the college and hinder experimentation (65%) (A)

Item b of this statement was the only autocratic response in the area of "Purpose of the College" to receive a reliable percentage vote. Fear of a powerful central authority administering a national college entrance policy breaks through the philosophic line of cleavage and gains commanding support in all groups and all classifications.

"Curriculum"

5. In the ranking of curriculum subjects, fine arts
    a. should have equal rank with the sciences, languages, and social and philosophic subjects (75%) (D)
    b. should be ranked below the sciences, languages, and social and philosophic subjects (23%)

On this statement the democratic response won a decisive majority over Item *b*, which inclined strongly toward the autocratic conception (.1005). All groups as to sex, control, type of student body, and geographical sections preferred the democratic response over Item *b* with reliable percentage differences.

10. As one basis for the revision of the college curriculum, a study of the prospective vocations of the students
    a. should be made and changes effected to meet their needs (65%) (D)
    b. is not essential (32%) (A)

No significant differences were found in the group votes on the items of this statement.

11. The college, through its curriculum and instruction, should
    a. teach only the prevailing social and economic doctrines (2%)
    b. present all doctrines, including the conservative and radical (84%) (D)
    c. adopt a definite social and economic doctrine and teach this doctrine with determination (13%) (A)

The democratic response was favored significantly by all groups in all classifications except one—the Roman Catholic group. The latter alone gave a majority vote for the autocratic response and alone showed a reliable percentage difference in its preference for the autocratic over the democratic response. The only other appreciable votes for Item *c* came from the men's college (39%) and 250 or less enrollment (28%) groups.

Groups giving 90%-100% support to the democratic response were: Control—public (93%), private (94%); Denomination—Congregational (100%), Methodist Episcopal (96%), Lutheran (92%), M. E. South (92%), Friends (100%), Brethern (100%), Disciples (100%); Size—1500-2000 (95%); 10,000 and over (100%); Type of Student Body—coeducational (91%); Geographical Sections—New England (96%), Mountain (91%); Race—Negro (100%).

"Improvement of Instruction"

2. The best teaching may be expected at the college level when
    a. there is close and constant guidance of instruction by the dean and heads of departments (22%)
    b. there is occasional suggestion from deans and heads of departments (62%) (D)
    c. each teacher is free to choose his own method and teach in his own way (14%)

All groups in all classifications gave their heaviest votes to the democratic response except the Congregational and Roman Catholic groups. The former cast a 50% vote for both Items *b* and *c*; the latter gave its highest vote to Item *a*.

Considerable minority support for Item *a* came from the following groups: Age—under 50 years (28%); Control—denominational (27%); Denomination—Roman Catholic (50%), Brethern (33%), Lutheran (31%), Methodist Episcopal (28%), Disciples (20%); Size—250 or less (28%), 500-750 (28%), 750-1000 (26%), 5000-10,000 (29%); Geographical Sections—East South Central (43%), Middle Atlantic (24%), West North Central (23%), West South Central (26%), Pacific (28%); Race—Negro (37%).

This analysis supports the opinion that while supervision on the college level is generally regarded as undesirable, there are spots where "close and constant guidance of instruction" is viewed with considerable favor.

3. In the proper evaluation of methods
   a. the experience of our best college teachers is sufficient criterion (25%) (A)
   b. experimentation should be made to determine proper criteria (70%) (D)

All age and control groups showed a significant preference for the democratic over the autocratic response. The geographical sections showed a preference for Item *b*, but in varying proportions. The Mountain group gave it the highest percentage (91%) and the Pacific group the lowest (52%). The strongest support for the autocratic response came from the Pacific (43%), New England (35%), Middle Atlantic (32%), and South Atlantic (32%) groups.

17. The chief concern of a college instructor should be
    a. to present his subject in well-organized form to his students (7%) (A)
    b. to make sure, by tests, etc., that his students have mastered the facts and principles of his course (5%) (A)
    c. to aid the student in growing by reason of his pursuit of this particular course (85%) (D)

No significant differences were found in the analysis of votes on this statement. All groups favored the democratic response. The chief support for the autocratic responses came from these groups: Control—public (15%); Geographical Sections—New England (13%), Middle Atlantic (17%), South Atlantic (14%), Pacific (14%).

"Student Welfare"

1. In higher education, as in elementary and secondary education
   a. there should be equality of opportunity to secure a suitable education (69%) (D)
   b. equality of opportunity is not essential (22%) (A)
   c. equality of opportunity is detrimental (6%)

No significant differences appeared in the votes on this statement. All groups except the Congregational and Roman Catholic gave their largest votes to the democratic response. These two groups gave their chief support to the autocratic response.

4. The policy of the college toward students who cannot maintain a creditable standard of scholarship under existing curricula should be to
   a. force them to leave (59%) (A)
   b. establish courses and curricula for their special benefit (37%) (D)

In this instance the autocratic response won a reliable percentage. The groups emphatically favoring it were: Sex—female (77%); Denomination—Presbyterian (82%), Baptist (75%), Lutheran (85%), M. E. South (77%), Friends (83%), Brethern (100%); Type of Student Body—men's colleges (77%), women's colleges (73%); Geographical Sections—New England (88%), East North Central (73%).

The notable statistically significant percentage differences in the votes on this statement were:

a) Preference of the Roman Catholic group for Item *b* over Item *a*, as compared with similar preferences of the Presbyterian, Baptist, Lutheran, M. E. South, Friends, Brethern, and of all Protestant groups combined;

b) Preference of the public group for Item *b* over Item *a*, when compared with similar preferences of the private and denominational groups;

c) Preference of the coeducational group for Item *b* over Item *a*, when compared with similar preferences of the men's college and women's college groups;

d) Preference of the West South Central and Mountain sections for Item *b* over Item *a*, when compared with similar preferences of the New England, Middle Atlantic and East North Central groups;

e) Preference of the West North Central, South Atlantic, East South Central and Pacific groups for Item *b* over Item *a*, when compared with the similar preference of the New England group.

6. Before admission a college should know a student's
   a. I.Q. only (¼%)
   b. I.Q. and previous school grades (2%)
   c. I.Q., previous school grades, and character traits (12%) (A)
   d. all possible cumulative information about the student (85%) (D)

Percentage differences in favor of the democratic response over all other items, both separately and combined, were reliable for all groups in their votes on this statement. No significant differences appeared among the groups.

11. Observance of Freshman Week
    a. yields important values (72%) (D)
    b. is of little or no value (25%) (A)

On this statement the democratic response received the majority vote of all groups in all classifications except the Pacific group. The autocratic response drew its chief support from the following groups: Denomination—Presbyterian (36%), Baptist (34%); Size—250 or less (36%), 1500-2000 (35%), 2000-5000 (33%), 5000-10,000 (43%), 10,000 and over (33%); Geographical Sections—Pacific (52%), West South Central (37%). The preferences of all other groups for the democratic over the autocratic response were statistically significant.

The enrollment groups of 250 to 1500 seem to sense considerable more value in Freshman Week than do enrollment groups below and above those limits. The same observation holds for private and denominational groups as compared with the public group.

12. Orientation courses in the Freshman and Sophomore years have proved
    a. of little if any value (25%) (A)
    b. of considerable value (59%) (D)
    c. extremely valuable (9%) (D)

The combined votes of the two democratic responses reveal that 68% of the deans participating in this study find considerable value in Orientation Courses in the junior college years. In no instance did the autocratic response have a clear lead in the tabulation. Its chief support came from the following groups: Control—private (36%), denominational (34%); Denomination—Disciples (40%); Size—750-1000 (32%), 10,000 and over

(33%); Geographical Sections—New England (35%), Middle Atlantic (31%), Pacific (43%). The preferences of all other groups for the combined democratic responses over the autocratic were statistically significant.

17. A college should properly consider among its responsibilities
　　a. the placement of its graduates (14%) (D)
　　b. the placement and follow-up of its graduates (73%) (A)
　　c. neither the placement nor follow-up of its graduates (10%)

All groups in all classifications gave their high or highest votes to the autocratic response. The only groups not expressing a significant preference for Item b over Items a and c respectively were the 2000-5000 enrollment, 5000-10,000 enrollment and Pacific groups. The preferences of all groups for Items a and b combined (placement) showed reliable percentage differences when compared with their preferences for Item c.

A commanding percentage of deans reporting in this study (87%) consider the placement of its graduates a responsibilty of the college, and a reliable percentage further believe that the follow-up of these graduates is a like responsibility. A slight tendency is noted among the groups of largest enrollments and the eastern and far-west geographical sections to disclaim responsibility for both placement and follow-up.

22. Student criticism is valuable in the determination of college policies chiefly because
　　a. the student is generally fair in his criticism (2%) (A)
　　b. the student is in the best position to know his own needs (0%)
　　c. the student's point of view forms a good supplement to the faculty point of view (97%) (D)

No significant differences were found in the votes on this statement.

SCORES OF GROUP OF DEANS ON SELECTED SECTIONS OF TWO TESTS

The scores of the group of deans participating in this study, on 330 instruments and 237 "Tests on Controversial Issues," were computed for the sections of the instruments that revealed the following viewpoints: Democratic Administration, Classic-Centered, Professional-Centered, Experience-Centered, Administration-Centered, Classroom Teaching-Centered, and Research-Centered. The means, sigmas, adjusted means and adjusted sigmas are presented in Table 22. The adjusted means and sigmas represent per cents on a scale from zero to 100 and are therefore readily compared.

TABLE 22

SCORES OF GROUP OF DEANS ON SEVEN SELECTED SECTIONS OF TESTS

Viewpoint	Mean	Sigma	Adjusted Mean (%)	Adjusted Sigma (%)
Democratic Administration*..	8.71	7.21	70.	12.4
Classic-Centered	16.43	2.76	13.0	6.0
Professional-Centered	16.13	3.31	20	9.8
Experience-Centered	5.29	3.95	53	9.8
Administration-Centered	2.56	2.94	55	7.9
Classroom Teaching-Centered.	7.13	3.12	61	6.5
Research-Centered	−.035	3.06	35	8.3

* For group of 330 deans. All other data in this table are for group of 237 deans of the total group.

Statistical treatment confirms the conclusion that the group of 330 deans participating in this study is definitely inclined toward the democratic conception of college administration. The adjusted means presented in Table 22 indicate, also, that this group of 237 deans is more Experience-Centered than either Professional-Centered or Classic-Centered; is more inclined toward Administration and Classroom Teaching than toward Research. As between Administration and Classroom Teaching, there is a slight leaning toward the latter.

Further statistical comparison of this group of 237 deans is possible since scores for five other groups on the "Test on Controversial Issues" have been computed. The members of these groups were, at the time of marking the instrument, graduate students in the following departments of Teachers College: Higher Education, Advisers of Women, Secondary Education, Educational Economics. The fifth group consists of the total of these four groups.

For greater ease of comparison, the adjusted means and sigmas for these groups are presented side by side in Table 23.

Table 23 indicates that the deans, as a group, are decidedly less Classic-Centered and slightly less Professional-Centered and Experience-Centered than all of the other groups compared. They seem, also, less Research-Centered, but no noticeable difference appears as to Administration or Classroom Teaching.

TABLE 23

SCORES OF GROUPS OF DEANS AND OF GRADUATE STUDENTS IN FOUR DEPART-
MENTS OF TEACHERS COLLEGE ON SIX SELECTED SECTIONS OF TEST*

Viewpoint		Adj. Scores (%)	(237) Deans	Higher Educ. (77)	Advisers of Women (110)	Sec. Educ. (127)	Ed. Econ. (41)	Total St. Groups (355)
Classic-	Mean	13.0	38.	34.	30	33	33
Centered	Sigma	6.0	9.83	9.89	9.35	9.15	10.07
Professional-	Mean	20	29.0	30	31	31	30
Centered	Sigma	9.8	10.21	10.98	13.64	11.00	11.89
Experience-	Mean	53	66	67	62	69	65
Centered	Sigma	9.8	11.29	9.20	9.04	11.18	10.18
Administration-	Mean	55	56	59	59	54	57
Centered	Sigma	7.9	8.37	9.63	8.79	9.26	9.16
Classroom	Mean	61	66	65	63	66	65
Teaching-	Sigma	6.5	8.16	8.67	8.94	7.18	8.63
Centered							
Research-	Mean	35	43	45	46	50	46
Centered	Sigma	8.3	10.05	9.25	9.50	9.35	9.75

* Data for all groups except the deans are furnished by Dr. D. P. Cottrell from unpublished
manuscript.

CORRELATIONS OF SCORES ON TRAITS

Correlations were run between the various scores on the 237
returned forms of the "Test on Controversial Issues" and the
"democratic" and "autocratic" self-rated scores of the same individuals on the instrument.

The correlations were found to be as follows:

Viewpoint	r	PE_r
Democratic with Classic-Centered	+.078	±.04
Autocratic with Classic-Centered	−.003	±.04
Democratic with Professional-Centered	+.068	±.04
Autocratic with Professional-Centered	−.13	±.04
Democratic with Experience-Centered	+.147	±.04
Autocratic with Experience-Centered	−.146	±.04
Democratic with Administration	−.092	±.04
Autocratic with Administration	+.125	±.04
Democratic with Classroom Teaching	+.37	±.04
Autocratic with Classroom Teaching	−.30	±.04
Democratic with Research	+.025	±.04
Autocratic with Research	−.03	±.04

As the data reveal, none of these correlations were sufficiently high to denote positive association. The highest positive correlation ($+.37 \pm .04$) was between the "democratic" conception and "classroom teaching"; the highest negative correlation ($-.30 \pm .04$) between the "autocratic" conception and "classroom teaching." To the degree in which these r's are reliable, the former would indicate that the deans who prefer classroom teaching are inclined to the democratic conception of college administration; the latter would indicate that the deans of this group who do not prefer classroom teaching are inclined toward the autocratic conception of college administration.

GROUP SCORES ON SIGNIFICANT ITEMS

The votes of the groups, in their choice of the various significant democratic and autocratic items of the instrument, are presented as totals in Table 24.

Considering the point balance or final score, as shown in Table 24, no noticeable difference appears among the groups as to age. As to sex, the democratic balance is slightly higher for the male than female, which corresponds with the indications from both the percentage and the Yule formula process. As to control, the private group shows the lowest democratic balance. Among the denominations, the Roman Catholic alone has a balance in the autocratic column, which agrees with the findings of the Yule formula and the percentage difference method.

The 2,000-5,000 enrollment group shows no balance in either column and, together with the 250 or less, 5,000-10,000 and 10,000 and over enrollment groups, shows no strong democratic leaning. This agrees with the Yule formula indications in respect to the 2,000-5,000 and 5,000-10,000 enrollment groups, and with the percentage method findings on all groups except the largest.

The order of rank, democratically, as indicated for the coeducational, women's college and men's college groups, conforms exactly with the order of rank indicated by both the Yule formula and percentage method.

New England and Pacific groups are low in the democratic column, which indication agrees with the Yule formula and percentage method findings. The racial difference is also indicated by the Yule formula method.

In brief, the conclusions indicated by the three methods of

TABLE 24

TOTAL SIGNIFICANT DEMOCRATIC AND AUTOCRATIC ITEMS OF THE INSTRUMENTS
CHOSEN BY THE VARIOUS GROUPS OF 330 DEANS

	Group	No. of Items Chosen		Point Balance	
		Dem.	Aut.	Dem.	Aut.
Age	20–29	11	2	9	
	30–39	11	2	9	
	40–49	11	2	9	
	50–59	10	1	9	
	60–69	10	2	8	
	70–79	11	2	9	
	80–89	10	2	8	
Sex	Male	6	1	5	
	Female	5	2	3	
Control	Public	17	3	14	
	Private	15	5	10	
	Denominational	17	3	14	
Denomina-tions	Roman Catholic	7	8		1
	Presbyterian	11	5	6	
	Methodist Episcopal	12	3	9	
	Baptist	13	2	11	
	Lutheran	12	3	9	
	M. E. South	12	3	9	
	Friends	11	5	6	
	Brethren	13	4	9	
	Disciples	13	4	9	
	Congregational	12	8	4	
Size	250 or less	9	5	4	
	250–500	12	3	9	
	500–750	12	3	9	
	750–1000	12	4	8	
	1000–1500	13	3	10	
	1500–2000	13	2	11	
	2000–5000	7	7	0	0
	5000–10,000	11	8	3	
	10,000 and over	10	8	2	
Type of Stu-dent Body	Men's colleges	9	3	6	
	Women's colleges	9	2	7	
	Coeducational	10	2	8	
Geographical Section	New England	14	9	5	
	Middle Atlantic	17	4	13	
	East North Central	18	4	14	
	West North Central	18	2	16	
	South Atlantic	18	3	15	
	East South Central	18	2	16	
	West South Central	20	1	19	
	Mountain	18	2	16	
	Pacific	12	8	4	
Race	White	11	4	7	
	Negro	13	3	10	

treatment—percentage difference, Yule formula, and scoring key of instrument—are in substantial agreement.

SUMMARY

This chapter has presented the significant data obtained by the instrument devised for this study. These data were treated by a variety of statistical processes, the principal results of which were in general agreement, so far as classification of groups on the conception of college administration was concerned.

The method of determining a satisfactory minimum index of consensus was described. The significant democratic and autocratic items that secured a reliable percentage vote were then analyzed by both straight-counts and cross-counts, and important differences were reported in detail. They are too numerous to review in a brief summary. The major interpretations are formally stated in the following chapter on "Conclusions."

The conclusion that the group of 330 deans participating in this study is definitely inclined toward the democratic conception of college administration was confirmed by statistical treatment. The group of 237 deans was found to be more Experience-Centered than either Classic-Centered or Professional-Centered, and more inclined toward Administration and Classroom Teaching than Research. They were also found to be less Classic-Centered and less Research-Centered than five other groups of graduate students in Teachers College. Correlations failed to reveal any high degree of positive association between conception of college administration and six other traits tested in the "Test on Controversial Issues."

The number of democratic and autocratic items of the instrument chosen by each group, and the final score of each group, are presented in tabular form.

CHAPTER VII

Conclusions

ANALYSIS of the data presented in this study prompts the following conclusions, which are first stated categorically and then individually followed by comments as to their significance:

1. The office of college dean or dean of the faculty is a comparatively recent development in American higher education.

The range of sixty-three years in the dates of the establishment of deanships in 319 institutions, with the median date of 1913, is evidence of the late development of this office within colleges and universities of the United States. This recency of development constitutes a contributing factor to the confusion that at present attends the general organization and functioning of the deanship.

2. The deanship has developed in a haphazard fashion from widely differing causes and a variety of college offices.

Thirty-six different reasons were assigned by 289 institutions for the establishment of this office; thirty-four varying origins were reported by 317 colleges and universities. This haphazard course of development likewise constitutes a contributing factor to the present confusion in the organization and functioning of the office.

3. The deanship is now generally accepted as a necessary and essential administrative office in higher educational institutions.

This general acceptance on the part of more than three-fourths of the institutions of higher learning indicates that the experimental period for this office is ended, that it has definitely proved its worth, and that it has permanently won its place in the scheme of collegiate administration.

4. The office of dean now exists in practically 85% of the liberal arts colleges in the United States. The movement for its establishment continues in the larger institutions, with the strong probability that the saturation point has about been reached.

5. At the present time there is a distinct tendency in the small colleges to combine the offices of dean and registrar; in the larger institutions, to subordinate the office of registrar to that of dean.

This tendency among small colleges to combine the offices of dean and registrar, while partly accounted for by retrenchment demands, also indicates that the two separate offices may not be needed until a certain enrollment size is reached. Institutions of one hundred or less enrollment reporting in this study had, with but one exception, a single office. It is probable that in institutions whose enrollments do not exceed two hundred fifty students the work of the dean and registrar may conveniently be combined under one officer.

The tendency in the larger institutions to subordinate the office of registrar to that of dean evidences both the growing importance of the deanship and the responsibility of the office in the matter of student admissions.

6. The office of dean is still in the process of evolution, with no uniformity and little standardization. It continues to accept new responsibilities and is now delegating certain duties, such as discipline, records, absences, to new or subordinate offices.

7. The deans of the liberal arts colleges in the United States are, as a group, mature individuals.

The median age of fifty, while partly accounted for by a very creditable tenure record for the office, strongly indicates that liberal arts colleges generally desire maturity in the deanship as an assurance of proper handling of the heavy responsibilities of the office.

8. The great majority of liberal arts college deanships in the United States are held by men.

Of the forty-seven women deans reporting in this study, forty-four were in women's colleges and three in coeducational institutions. Present practice, therefore, seems definitely to limit the opportunities of women academic deans to women's colleges. The preference for men deans in coeducational institutions is unmistakable. This preference, however, is in line with the present practice in regard to certain other educational administrative positions, such as president of college, superintendent of schools, and, to a less degree, principal of senior high school.

9. Deans rank high academically, have traveled extensively, and frequently have studied in foreign institutions.

10. Of the subject-matter fields, science, social studies, English, and the education-philosophy-psychology fields yield by far the largest numbers of college deans.

This fact tends to refute the assumption often made that a very large percentage of deans are recruited from subject-matter fields of declining interest. It further indicates that such factors as small classes and light teaching loads are becoming much less influential in the appointment of deans.

11. In at least 50% of the cases the deans seem to have had less than a satisfactory preparation for the office. Scarcely half of the total number have had previous administrative experience, while comparatively few have taken professional courses preparing directly for the deanship.

In this connection it should again be noted that professional courses preparing directly for the deanship are new in the curricula of universities and are offered by only a few institutions at the present time. Opinion as to their value is sharply divided. In the absence of scientific evidence it seems wise to place major emphasis upon broad general and fundamental study of the problems of higher education as a whole, rather than upon specific techniques applicable to particular situations. Adequate theoretical and practical training of this type should, at the same time, increase the efficiency of college deans and enhance the importance of the office.

12. The tendency to confer the deanship in recognition of long service to the institution is rapidly diminishing.

The majority of the present deans in liberal arts colleges participating in this study have been on the staffs of their respective institutions less than ten years. Indications are strong that many colleges are choosing for this office men from outside the institution or of shorter experience within it. This is a significant development, indicating that long service itself is ceasing to be a major factor in the appointment of deans and that other more essential qualifications are being more and more required.

13. Deans are mature in point of educational experience.

The median total educational experience of the deans participating in this study was 23.27 years; the range was from 3 to 52 years. No deans in this study have been in educational work less than three years, only three less than six years, and only thirty-three less than ten years. This wealth of educational experience, of the right sort, should prove a real asset in the deanship.

14. The tenure of college deans exceeds the record of the usual college staff member.

This greater permanency in office makes for stabilization and should, in time, not only bring improvement to the organization and functioning of the administrative machinery of the college but also increasingly attract able men to the deanship.

15. The majority of deans favor the democratic conception of college administration.

This conclusion is confirmed by statistical treatment which locates the adjusted mean for the group of 330 deans included in this study at a point 70% toward the democratic end of the self-rating scale. It is further confirmed by the preponderant reliable percentage support for significant democratic item responses.

This marked favor of the total group of deans for the democratic conception of college administration indicates the strong probability that administration in liberal arts colleges is more democratic in practice than it is in form; it may, indeed, be prophetic of a growing democracy in administrative practices of institutions of higher learning which may, in time, approximate the philosophy proposed in the final chapter of this study.

16. Groups that incline, either definitely or strongly, to the democratic conception of college administration are: Denomination—Presbyterian, Methodist Episcopal, Brethern, Disciples; Type of Student Body—Coeducational; Geographical Sections—West South Central, West North Central, Mountain.

All nine Protestant denominational college groups incline toward the democratic conception, in varying degrees, the four listed above showing the strongest preferences in this direction. The shorter tradition of Protestantism, the more or less decentralized forms of their church governments, and their close contact with the spirit of democracy as exemplified in the United States and the British Isles may largely account for the democratic leanings of these nine denominations.

The coeducational college group likewise definitely inclines toward the democratic conception of college administration. Coeducation in the United States was largely a product of the growing spirit of democracy in the western hemisphere which clashed not only with the tradition of educational segregation of the sexes but also with the practice of educational submergence of women. Acceptance of the principle of equality of sex, which developed through successive stages, made coeducation a natural resultant. The increased use of public tax funds for the purposes of higher education, as exemplified in state colleges and state universities, gave added impetus to the coeducational idea. In this democratic environment it was only natural that the democratic conception of college administration would take firm root and grow rapidly.

The interior geographical sections of the United States, as represented by their college groups, are also democratically inclined. These sections were successive homes of the moving frontier. The American pioneer was fundamentally a democrat. Institutions of learning which he supported or which came in his wake would perforce be indelibly tinged with his democratic philosophy. Moreover, the Protestant denominations, which founded and financially supported a very large per cent of the colleges throughout these areas, were in more or less degree democratically organized and administered. In most of this territory education was from the start, particularly on the lower levels, publicly-supported. Private education never gained the foothold in the central and western sections that it did along the Atlantic seaboard. Here was an atmosphere charged with democracy from the very beginning, and its influence is distinctly reflected in the thinking of administrators of colleges in these areas today.

No noticeable preference for the democratic conception of college administration appears among the groups classified on the basis of age. As to sex, while the male group showed stronger preference for the democratic conception than the female, this is doubtless accounted for by the fact that all but three of the forty-seven women deans are in women's colleges, mostly private, which group was preponderantly autocratic. As to race, the Negro college deans showed a stronger preference for democratic administration than the white group. In all probability, however, the characteristic of race had little if anything to do with the establishment of this preference. Of the nineteen Negro colleges, only two were private while two were public, one national, and fourteen Protestant denominational; only two were men's colleges while seventeen were coeducational; none were located in the New England or Pacific sections. Indications are that the larger per cent of private colleges, of men's and women's colleges, of Roman Catholic colleges, and of New England and Pacific group colleges in the white group account principally for the variation between the Negro and white groups in the matter of preference for the democratic conception of college administration.

17. Groups that incline, either definitely or strongly, to the autocratic conception of college administration are: Denomination —Roman Catholic; Size—2000-5000, 5000-10,000; Type of Student Body—Men's College, Women's College; Geographical Sections—New England, Pacific.

Throughout the study the group of deans of Roman Catholic colleges showed a decisive preference for the autocratic conception of college administration. This is in harmony with the type of organization of their church government, which has for centuries been a highly centralized one. As the church founded schools for the fostering of education this principle of centralization of authority followed through into the educational administrative practices and persists today with much the same emphasis.

Institutions whose enrollments ranged between 2000 and 10,000 expressed, through the group of deans, a preference for the autocratic conception. This was particularly true of the seven institutions with enrollments between 5000 and 10,000. The three institutions, however, of more than 10,000 enrollment inclined toward the democratic theory, but their number is too small to prompt a conclusion. There is a strong probability that increasing enrollments in the larger institutions—2000 or more—tend to be accompanied by the development of more complicated administrative machinery which may easily incline toward the autocratic method. Exceptions, such as at the University of Michigan, prove that this course is not necessarily inevitable, though it is doubtless true that greater effort must be made in the larger and more complicated situations if the democratic type of administration is to prevail.

The Men's College and Women's College groups definitely preferred the autocratic type of administration. This may be largely accounted for by the fact that the great majority of these institutions are of private origin and under private control or under the direction of the Roman Catholic Church. They are, also, principally centered in the East, where the autocratic principle finds its greatest educational strength. Moreover, the theory of segregation of sexes harmonizes more readily with the conservative or autocratic conception than with the democratic administrative practice.

The New England and Pacific groups were the only geographical sections to show distinct preference for autocratic administration in colleges. The conservative tradition of New England, borrowed quite largely from European sources, together with the growth and persistence of private educational agencies, materially assists in preserving the autocratic principle of administration in this section.

The similar preference of the Pacific group is not so easily understood. This section, however, has been influenced by New England more than the casual observer would detect. History records that during the migration period many New Englanders went directly to the western coast. They carried with them their New England educational ideals. Furthermore, many higher institutions of learning were founded along the western coast by the Roman Catholic Church and many of these Pacific group institutions have large enrollments. There seems, therefore, considerable similarity in the thinking along administrative lines of the deans of the New England and Pacific college groups.

18. In this study the Roman Catholic group shows a stronger preference for the autocratic conception of college administration than do any of the nine following denominational groups, either separately or combined: Presbyterian, Methodist Episcopal, Baptist, Lutheran, M.E. South, Friends, Brethern, Disciples, Congregational.

If the purpose of the institution is indoctrination of its students in certain creeds and theologies held by the various denominations, it is highly probable that the autocratic type of college administration would more completely effect this end than would the democratic conception. Where a predetermined pattern is desired, the autocratic administrative practice is admirably designed to achieve this pattern. On the other hand, however, the question arises whether such a policy so administered permits proper respect for the personalities of the students themselves or supplies conditions conducive to the fullest development of all their powers and abilities. If indoctrination in certain beliefs and fullest development of abilities of students cannot both be attained by the same administrative process, that fact should be recognized, though it remains the privilege of the institution to define its particular purpose.

19. As revealed by the scores on the "Test on Controversial Issues," the group of 237 deans is more Experience-Centered than either Classic-Centered or Professional-Centered, and more inclined toward Administration and Classroom Teaching than Research. It is less Classic-Centered and less Research-Centered than five graduate student groups of Teachers College, Columbia University, as revealed by comparative scores.

In this connection the term "Classic-Centered" may be defined as acceptance of the theory that the most valuable kind of education for college students is that which is concerned primarily with the great masterpieces constituting our cultural heritage as selected by expert scholars and taught by expert instructors, the measure of the success of the student being the degree in which he has mastered these selected subjects of study in literature, science, art, philosophy, etc.

"Professional-Centered" means acceptance of the theory that the most valuable kind of education for college students today is that which is concerned primarily with the materials leading to the direct preparation of the student for his life-work, these materials to be selected by persons of recognized ability to judge what is needed by workers in the several professions and to be mastered by the student, the measure of his success being the degree in which he attains the skills and achieves the standards of proficiency generally recognized as prerequisite to final qualification for practice in that profession.

"Experience-Centered" means acceptance of the theory that the most valuable kind of education for college students today is that which is concerned primarily with the interests and felt needs (particularly those of great social importance) of the students themselves, these educational activities to be selected by the students for the discovery of educationally significant interests and reconsideration of convictions and viewpoints, the measure of success being the degree in which the students have, in the judgment of their teachers, attained the objectives agreed upon by students and teachers from time to time during the course of the college work.

"Administration-Centered" may be defined as a dominant interest in administrative tasks because of basic satisfactions derived therefrom.

"Classroom-Teaching-Centered" is defined as a dominant interest in classroom teaching because of basic satisfactions thereby afforded.

"Research-Centered" is defined as a dominant interest in the prosecution of research work because of basic satisfactions accruing therefrom.

The group of 237 deans in this study indicated, by their favor for the "Experience-Centered" position, a preference for the theory that the most valuable kind of education for college students today is that which is concerned primarily with the students' own interests and felt needs (particularly those of great social importance); that the students in consultation with their instructors should choose educational activities designed to assist them in discovering educationally significant interests and in reconsidering and reconstructing their own convictions and viewpoints; that if any formal measure of success is required it should be the degree in which the teachers feel that the students have attained the objectives determined by the students and teachers from time to time during the college course. This strong preference for the "Experience-Centered" position over both the "Professional Centered" and the "Classic-Centered" positions indicates the democratic tendency of the group in that it desires to give proper consideration to the judgments and interests of the students.

Of singular interest is the finding that this group of administrators finds its greatest basic satisfactions in classroom teaching. While this may be largely accounted for by the fact that most of these deans were formerly classroom teachers and are now, as one writer has put it, "professors on parole," it also indicates their very deep interest in the problems of instruction and is a condition that should prove conducive to the much-needed improvement of classroom teaching on the college level.

That these deans should also show a strong interest in administration was to be expected. Derivation by them of great basic satisfactions from the performance of administrative duties makes not only for efficiency but also for greater permanency in office.

The rather slight interest of this group in research may be an item of considerable significance. If democracy in administration is to be achieved, research must be an agency in that achievement and a condition of its continuance. Traditional autocratic forms will not be set aside unless experimentation discloses indisputable evidence to support more democratic procedures. Furthermore, democracy and research should go hand in hand. Democracy is somehow the element in which experimentation best thrives. It allows for greater freedom and encourages initiative and individuality. It has less reverence for the old and less fear of the new. It is willing to try new theories, and if the theories are correct they must be made to work in practice. The democratic principle, for instance, believed by many progressive educators, that on the college level provision must be made for participation in the making of an administrative policy by all who are affected by it, must be proved in actual practice. Experimentation is the indispensable agency in this proving process.

Since direction of research is considered a major responsibility of the dean of the faculty, it is of increased importance that he have a real interest in research. In the undergraduate institution the research program may well be a limited one, but there should be such a program. The institution itself should be under constant study—its curriculum, its methods of instruction, the performance and progress of its students, etc. For a college to perform its mission in the most creditable manner requires a research program of which the dean seems the logical director.

20. So far as correlations indicate, in reference to this group of 237 deans, there is no high degree of positive association between preference for the democratic or the autocratic conception of college administration and any of the following traits: Classic-Centeredness, Professional-Centeredness, Experience-Centeredness, Administration-Centeredness, Classroom-Teaching-Centeredness, Research-Centeredness.

The highest positive association was found to be between Democratic Conception of Administration and Experience-Centeredness

($+$ .147 $\pm$ .04) ; the highest negative correlation between Autocratic Conception of Administration and Experience-Centeredness ($-$ .146 $\pm$ .04). There is, therefore, no statistical evidence in this study to show definite association between any two individual traits in these different categories. In other words, the dean who favors the "democratic conception of administration" is almost as apt to be "classic-centered" or "professional-centered" as "experience-centered," and the dean who favors the "autocratic conception of administration" is almost as apt to be "professional-centered" or "experience-centered" as "classic-centered."

In the other group of traits, the highest positive association was found to be between the Democratic Conception of Administration and Classroom Teaching ($+$ .37 $\pm$ .04) ; the highest negative correlation between the Autocratic Conception of Administration and Classroom Teaching ($-$ .30 $\pm$ .04). Only in this very slight degree is it indicated that deans who prefer "classroom teaching" are inclined to the "democratic conception of administration" and that deans who do not prefer "classroom teaching" incline toward the "autocratic conception of administration." The democratically-inclined dean is as apt to prefer "administration" as "research," and the same is true of the autocratically-inclined dean.

21. The deans of the liberal arts colleges are in substantial agreement, confirmed by a reliable percentage, upon the starred(*) alternatives to forty-three statements in regard to higher education. It should be repeated in this connection that the alternatives to statements were not designed to be mutually exclusive in all instances. Therefore, in the case of certain statements it was taken for granted that the individual marking the instrument would be in some agreement with more than one alternative, and might not be in complete agreement with any single alternative offered. But his selection of one alternative would indicate his preference for the one over the others, and would express the point of his emphasis. This selection, however, discriminated only as to the specific alternatives offered in the instrument. Through this method of marking it was possible to determine the opinions of the total group of 330 deans on the various controversial issues set forth in the instrument of this study.

The forty-three statements with their accompanying alternatives follow :

Conclusions

1. The purpose of the liberal arts college in the United States
       a. is now sufficiently definite and adequately understood.
      b. definitely needs clarification at this time.
2. The purpose of a liberal arts college
      a. should adapt itself to the present needs of students.
       b. should change only if the supporting constituency changes.
       c. should generally remain permanent during the life of the institution.
3. Higher education will best be developed and improved by
       a. continuing the present competitive processes among colleges.
      b. eliminating these competitive processes and establishing voluntary cooperative agencies.
4. The strongest influences toward reform in college education must come
       a. from new educational philosophies sponsored by laymen.
       b. from student pressure.
      c. from college administrative and professional forces.
5. The purpose of a college can best be realized by placing the responsibility for internal administration
       a. entirely in the hands of the president and board of trustees.
       b. entirely in the hands of the president, deans and executive officers.
      c. in the hands of the administrators and faculty in coöperation.
       d. in the hands of the faculty alone.
6. As social and economic needs have recently developed the college
      a. has generally lagged behind them.
       b. has kept pace with them.
       c. has anticipated them.
7. The liberal arts college of the future
       a. should continue to conserve and transmit classical knowledge.
       b. should become more professional and vocational in character.
      c. should endeavor to foster experiences for the rounded development of its students.
8. The primary effect of a national educational college entrance policy would be to
       a. eliminate wasteful competition and overlapping.
      b. give too much power to a central authority, thus tending to stereotype the college and hinder experimentation.
9. The definitely required courses in the college curriculum should
       a. be entirely abolished.
       b. include only "tool" subjects.
      c. include both "tool" and cultural subjects.
10. In the ranking of curriculum subjects, fine arts should
      a. have equal rank with the sciences, languages, and social and philosophic subjects.
       b. be ranked below the sciences, languages and social and philosophic subjects.
11. Of the following plans, the most effective educational organization of a college to secure the aims of liberal education is
       a. organization of the entire college as one unit.
      b. an organization with a few (four or five) major divisions.
       c. the present organization into departments.

12. From the viewpoint of quality of the educational process, the development of large, coördinated divisions in the college is
    *a. an improvement over the departmentalized organization.
    b. of equal effectiveness with the department system.
    c. definitely inferior to the system of departments.

13. In the revision of the curriculum, the dean of the faculty
    a. should leave it entirely to the subject-matter specialists.
    b. should serve only as a presiding officer during the process.
    *c. should initiate and actively guide the movement.

14. As one basis for the revision of the college curriculum, a study of the prospective vocations of the students
    *a. should be made and changes effected to meet their needs.
    b. is not essential.

15. The college, through its curriculum and instruction, should
    a. teach only the prevailing social and economic doctrines.
    *b. present all doctrines, including the conservative and radical.
    c. adopt a definite social and economic doctrine and teach this doctrine with determination.

16. As a general rule, the best type of instruction at the college level
    a. is individualized teaching.
    *b. may be either individualized or group teaching, as determined by conditions and subjects.

17. The best teaching may be expected at the college level when
    a. there is close and constant guidance of instruction by the dean and heads of departments.
    *b. there is occasional suggestion from deans and heads of departments.
    c. each teacher is free to choose his own method and teach in his own way.

18. In the proper evaluation of methods
    a. the experience of our best college teachers is sufficient criterion.
    *b. experimentation should be made to determine proper criteria.

19. As a rule, the student in literary fields develops best under a program of instruction based upon
    a. the individual plan (tutorial or preceptorial).
    *b. the small-group conference plan.
    c. the lecture and quiz-section plan.

20. Instruction will be improved on the college level by
    *a. more frequent contact between instructor and student.
    b. less frequent contact between instructor and student.

21. Faculty and student conferences as a feature of the instructional method make
    a. no appreciable contribution to student learning.
    *b. for better student learning.

22. "Honors courses" should be open
    *a. only to students of high scholastic standing.
    b. to all students showing a deep interest in the field, regardless of scholastic standing.

23. In preparing examinations for college courses, the emphasis should be
    - a. on short answer, objective type tests.
    - b. on subjective, essay type tests.
    - *c. on subjective and objective type tests in some rational proportion.
24. The present policy of permitting a student to qualify for graduation by accumulating credit hours and quality grade points should be
    - a. continued.
    - *b. continued, but supplemented by comprehensive examinations in the student's major field in the senior year.
    - c. replaced entirely by a system of comprehensive examinations throughout.
25. In selecting a college instructor it is usually wiser to employ
    - a. one with thorough knowledge of his subject, even though weak in personality.
    - *b. one not so thoroughly prepared in subject-matter, but possessing ability to stimulate and inspire students.
26. College faculty members should be selected primarily on the ground of
    - *a. personality and teaching ability.
    - b. research ability and publications.
27. The chief concern of a college instructor should be
    - a. to present his subject in well-organized form to his students.
    - b. to make sure, by tests, etc., that his students have mastered the facts and principles of his course.
    - *c. to aid the student in growing by reason of his pursuit of this particular course.
28. Student rating of instructors is
    - a. of great value.
    - *b. of some value.
    - c. a positive detriment.
29. Where student rating of instructors is practiced, the instructor
    - *a. should have knowledge of his own rating.
    - b. should not have knowledge of his own rating.
30. Where student rating of instructors is used, it should be
    - a. very influential in determining the instructor's teaching ability.
    - *b. only slightly influential in determining the instructor's teaching ability.
31. In higher education, as in elementary and secondary education
    - *a. there should be equality of opportunity to secure suitable education.
    - b. equality of opportunity is not essential.
    - c. equality of opportunity is detrimental.
32. Provisions in the college curriculum for the mediocre student
    - *a. should be made.
    - b. should not be made.
33. The policy of the college toward students who cannot maintain a creditable standard of scholarship under existing curricula should be to
    - *a. force them to leave.
    - b. establish courses and curricula for their special benefit.

34. Before admission the college should know a student's
    a. I.Q. only.
    b. I.Q. and previous school grades.
    c. I.Q., previous school grades, and character traits.
    *d. all possible cumulative information about the student.
35. Other things being equal, preference in admission to college should be
    a. given students from urban areas.
    b. given students from rural areas.
    *c. given irrespective of home locality.
36. Observance of Freshman Week
    *a. yields important values.
    b. is of little or no value.
37. Orientation courses in the Freshman and Sophomore years have proved
    a. of little if any value.
    *b. of considerable value.
    c. extremely valuable.
38. Vocational guidance of the student is
    *a. a definite duty of the college.
    b. not a particular duty of the college.
39. As a general rule, it is better for students to choose their careers
    a. early and make that choice permanent.
    *b. early and keep the choice flexible.
    c. only when ready to specialize, and change later if advisable.
40. A college should properly consider among its responsibilities
    a. the placement of its graduates.
    *b. the placement and follow-up of its graduates.
    c. neither the placement nor follow-up of its graduates.
41. Student criticism is valuable in the determination of college policies chiefly because
    a. the student is generally fair in his criticism.
    b. the student is in the best position to know his own needs.
    *c. the student's point of view forms a good supplement to the faculty point of view.
42. The theory of the student and adviser working out together the best course for the student is
    *a. the ideal plan.
    b. good in principle but impractical.
    c. fallacious.
43. A primary aim of college administration should be to
    a. make the students conform, without exception, to a well-ordered administration.
    *b. adapt the administration, as much as feasible, to meet changing needs of students and a flexible curriculum.
    c. conform whole-heartedly to needs of students, even though administrative difficulties are thereby considerably increased.

The opinions of this group of 330 deans on certain controversial issues in higher education, as expressed by their selection of alternatives to the foregoing statements, may conveniently be grouped in seven categories: (1) purpose of liberal arts college, (2) reform and improvement of college, (3) admission policies, (4) curriculum, (5) instruction, (6) guidance, (7) administration.

Purpose of Liberal Arts College. The consensus of opinion of this group of deans is that the purpose of the liberal arts college needs now to be clarified and adapted to the present needs of its students.

Reform and Improvement of College. The group generally agrees that the liberal arts college has lagged behind social and economic needs, that reform must come about through exercise of the influence of administrative and professional forces within the colleges, that substitution of voluntary coöperative agencies for the present competitive processes among colleges should lead to definite improvement, and that in the future the college should definitely focus on the fostering of experiences for the rounded development of its students.

Admission Policies. The group feels that a national educational college entrance policy would, by reason of the centralization of authority, prove unwise and harmful. It also feels that no preference should be given either rural or urban students over the other in the matter of admission to college; that equality of opportunity to secure a suitable education should be open to all on the college level; that all possible information about the student should be obtained before his admission; that provision should be made for the mediocre student as well as for the superior; but that a student should be forced to leave in the event he is unable to maintain a creditable standard of scholarship under existing curricula.

Curriculum. It is the opinion of this group that fine arts should have equal rank with the sciences, languages, and social and philosophic subjects in the curriculum; that prescribed courses should include both "tool" and cultural subjects; that the dean should initiate and actively guide the process of curriculum revision, and that one basis for revision might well be a study of the prospective vocations of the students.

Instruction. The deans of this group generally agree that personality and teaching ability are the prime requisites of a college instructor; that student rating of instructors has some value and should be slightly influential in determining the instructor's teaching ability, but should be made known to the instructor; that either individualized or group teaching may be most effective, depending upon conditions and subjects; that occasional suggestion from deans and heads of departments as to instruction but not close supervision is most apt to secure the best teaching at the college level; that experimentation should be made to determine proper criteria for the evaluation of teaching methods; that more student-faculty conferences might be expected to improve instruction; that only high scholarship students should be admitted to "Honors Courses"; that subjective and objective type tests in some rational proportion are the more feasible measures of student achievement at this time; that comprehensive examinations in the student's major field in the senior year should supplement the present system of accumulation of credits for graduation; that all social and economic doctrines, both conservative and radical, should be presented to college students through instruction and curriculum.

Guidance. On the matter of guidance, the group definitely believes that considerable value lies in "Orientation Courses" and "Freshman Week"; that the student and instructor should together work out the curriculum for the individual student; that students should choose their careers early and keep the choice flexible; and that vocational guidance of students, and placement and follow-up of its graduates are definite responsibilities of the college.

Administration. In matters of administration this group of deans substantially agrees that an organization of a few (four or five) major divisions is probably the most effective educational organization for a college; that the responsibility for the internal administration should be in the hands of the administrators and faculty in coöperation; that in the formulation of college policies the student's point of view forms a good supplement to the faculty's point of view; and that college administration should adapt itself, as much as feasible, to meet the changing needs of the students.

22. Two things are necessary for the proper continued development of the office of dean: (1) a clear and concise definition of its authority and responsibilities; (2) appointment to this office of only those who are adequately qualified in scholarship, professional training and experience, and natural endowment of mind and heart.

CHAPTER VIII

An Emerging Conception of the Deanship

For the liberal arts college, as for society as a whole, the present is a period of transition. In the social order that follows this transition the college should play a vital part. Before it lie three courses that may be followed: (1) it may cling to the social and economic philosophy of the past and strive to preserve its principles of instruction and administration as inviolate as changing conditions permit; (2) it may adapt itself to the new conditions as they develop, stimulating a progressive reconstruction of the social order with no intention of predetermining the nature of the reconstruction; or (3) it may frankly avow its purpose and bend its energies deliberately to fashion the social order of the morrow.

In support of the first course of action, Dr. William C. Bagley, in his most recent publication, has written:

Paradoxical as it may seem, it is the conservative functions of education that are most significant in a period of profound change. . . .

A second function of education in eras of rapid change may be called a stabilizing function. 'The very time to avoid chaos in the schools is when something akin to chaos characterizes the social environment. The very time to emphasize in the schools the values that are relatively certain and stable is when the social environment is full of uncertainty and when standards are crumbling. . . .

If education is to be a stabilizing force it means that the school must discharge what is in effect a disciplinary function. The materials of instruction, the methods of teaching, and the life of the school as a social organization must exemplify and idealize consideration, coöperation, cheerfulness, fidelity to duty and to trust, courage and perseverance in the face of disappointment, aggressive effort toward doing the task that one's hand finds to do and doing it as well as one can, loyalty to friend and family and those for whom one is responsible, a sense of fact and a willingness to face facts, clear and honest thinking. These may not be eternal values, but one may venture a fairly confident prediction that they will be just as significant a thousand years from now as they have ever been in the past.

It should go without saying that modifications of the school curriculum are needed from time to time as science reveals new truths, as art creates new treasures, as society meets and solves new problems. Fundamental and general education on the elementary and secondary levels should prepare the coming adult society to solve its problems not primarily by essaying the impossible task of predicting them, except as one may assume that there will be persistent problems, discussion of some of which may be profitable on the lower educational levels, but rather by equipping the young with the necessary skills and with the most reliable knowledge that the past has produced and that the young can assimilate, and by exemplifying and idealizing the traits named in the preceding paragraph. . . .

With qualifications set forth in Chapter XII, it is safe to conclude that it would be unwise to overload the programs of the lower schools and even of the earlier college years with materials from the inexact sciences and at the expense of the exact and exacting.[1]

The second course of action is urged by Dr. B. H. Bode, who writes:

The primary concern of a democratic educational procedure is to stimulate a reconstruction of our beliefs and habits in the light of their mutual relationships rather than to predetermine the nature of this reconstruction. The reconstruction will gravitate naturally and inevitably toward a philosophy of life or a social outlook, and it will take place with such assistance and encouragement as the schools can provide, but not according to any prescribed pattern. . . . All education, whether "liberal" or "technical," should help to create a sense that our traditions require reconstruction and thus provide community of understandings and interests, regardless of its content. In so doing it widens the areas of common purposes by weakening the antagonisms that spring from complacent short-sightedness and from stupid loyalties to the past. Real education humanizes men. It does so, however, not by moulding them into unthinking acceptance of preestablished patterns, but by stimulating them to a continuous reconstruction of their outlook on life.[2]

The genius of democracy expresses itself precisely in this continuous remaking of the social fabric. With regard to curriculum construction it requires, first of all, a type of education that enables the individual, not only to adapt himself to the existing social order, but to take part in its remaking in the interests of a greater freedom.[3]

Generally accepting this same viewpoint, Dean J. B. Johnston of the University of Minnesota, writes:

As we have seen, the intellectually capable classes are the ones on whom must fall the duty of recognizing the changed conditions and planning new policies which are needed to protect and forward human welfare. The college is the one institution in society which can train these persons to per-

[1] Bagley, W. C., *Education and Emergent Man*, pp. 154-159. (By permission of Thomas Nelson and Sons.)

[2] Bode, B. H., *The Educational Frontier*, Chap. I, pp. 29ff. (By permission of The Century Co.)

[3] Bode, B. H., *Modern Educational Theories*, pp. 19f.

form this service. In a very true sense this is the heart and core of the function of the college. The central purpose in making learning available is to enable society to adjust itself with the minimum friction and loss in successive stages of its evolution. This being so, the character and attitude of the college follows: The faculty and officers who determine its policies, should be aware of this most vital function and take care to facilitate its work of criticism, of scrutiny of social evolution, of analysis of new forces and changed conditions, of anticipation of the effect of these in human life, of social experimentation, of the examination of hypothetical procedures in industry, social customs, or political organization to meet the needs arising from changed conditions. . . . The welfare of the present and succeeding generations demands in the college both freedom of teaching and the conscious recognition of the duty to provide for the modification, rebuilding or replacement of the social institutions as this becomes necessary, and promptly enough to avoid confusion, conflict or catastrophe.

In other words, while education in general is primarily conservative, it is the business of the college to be consciously progressive.[4]

President L. D. Coffman, of the University of Minnesota, voices much the same belief in the following words:

It is my opinion that the universities of America never had such a unique opportunity as they now possess to serve the society of which they are a part and upon which they must rely for support. Not long ago I heard a distinguished Scotchman pride himself on the fact that the particular university with which he is associated had remained unchanged for nearly four hundred years. There it sat on top of the hill, a beacon light, so to speak, to all of the wayfarers in the valley below. It had a fine conception of scholarship of a traditional type. Its atmosphere breathed the spirit of learning, a spirit of learning, however, that was dedicated largely to the past. I do not feel that we should lose sight of the picture which this Scotchman drew. On the other hand, I am of the opinion that American universities will fail tragically if they keep their faces turned to the past. Surely they cannot ignore the sweeping changes that are going on all about them; they cannot set themselves apart from the life that sustains them. They may guide that life to some extent, but the guidance that they give should be guidance by men and women who are saturated with the spirit of science, who are capable of studying the facts of life for the sake of arriving at the truth, and who are willing to state the truth, regardless of the institutions or the individuals it may affect.[5]

Outstanding among those who favor the third course of action—deliberate fashioning, through the school, of a new social order—is Dr. George S. Counts. He speaks in no uncertain language when he questions if the school dare build a new social order.

    [4] Johnston, J. B., *The Liberal College in Changing Society*, pp. 36-39. (By permission of The Century Co.)
    [5] Coffman, L. D., "The Administration of Research During the Depression," *Journal of Higher Education*, Vol. 5, No. 1, p. 6, January, 1934.

We shall assume, as basic to the selection and evaluation of the activities of the college, that the larger outcome of a college education is to create in the student an understanding and appreciation of the principles upon which must be reared that society and that civilization for which the clear in mind and the pure in heart are continually striving. . . .

Put in another way, the aim of the college must be to train leaders who will be capable of viewing broadly and disinterestedly the problem of a co-operative society; leaders who will rise above class interests and class prejudices, who will be dominated by a spirit of service, who honestly and courageously will tread the paths which lead to progress.[6]

In the last analysis, the building of a new society must assume the prosaic garb of education. To shout revolutionary slogans, to conquer military and political power, to fashion broad plans of social change are clearly not enough. Unless the habits, the attitudes, the ideas, and the dispositions of the people are altered, unless the gap between the generations is greatly and consciously widened, unless children cease to follow in the footsteps of their parents, the new social order will never appear in the world of real things: it will possess no more permanence than the small band of idealists who conceived it and will perish with them. The failure of revolutions is a record of the failure to bring education into the service of the revolutionary cause.[7]

While the Dewey philosophy of Experimentalism may be said to be the dominant educational philosophy in the United States today, inasmuch as professors of education generally accept it, the actual practices in the schools of America are, in the main, preponderantly traditional. Counts finds the existing school in the grip of conservative forces.

That the existing school is leading the way to a better social order is a thesis which few informed persons would care to defend. Except as it is forced to fight for its own life during times of depression, its course is too serene and untroubled. Only in the rarest of instances does it wage war on behalf of principle or ideal. Almost everywhere it is in the grip of conservative forces and is serving the cause of perpetuating ideas and institutions suited to an age that is gone.[8]

Dr. H. H. Horn likewise feels that the conservatism of the teaching profession as a whole is depriving society of that leadership so sorely required and which only educated minds can give.

As a class are we not in bondage to tradition? We are among the conservative members of society. We teach what is known, the present and past, mainly the past. The goal toward which we are, or ought to be,

[6] Chapman, J. C., and Counts, George S., *Principles of Education*, pp. 486f. (By permission of Houghton Mifflin Company.)

[7] Counts, George S., *The Soviet Challenge to America*, p. 66. (By permission of The John Day Company.)

[8] Counts, George S., *Dare the School Build a New Social Order?* p. 5. (By permission of The John Day Company.)

moving rarely comes within our ken. We have not awakened to our work as a great constructive effort to shape developing society toward its true goal. Instead, we hand down traditional knowledge and socially-standardized viewpoints. The school does not lead social progress, it hardly keeps up with it. It ought to be developing social leadership and not merely conservative following. We should communicate, not merely established knowledge, but also ideas regarding the end and means of social progress. Society requires guidance as well as information.[9]

The faith of the American people in education is still an abiding faith. It is fair to assume that they desire their educational institutions to function effectively and coöperatively in an emerging society; that they wish their colleges and universities to assist in the fullest realization of the ideals of American democracy. For the rich development of personality and the intense stimulation of thought in the students who now enter their halls of learning, the colleges have a paramount responsibility. That many institutions are now realizing this responsibility and attempting, as best they can, to discharge this duty successfully is evidenced by the numerous experiments in operation throughout the field of higher education.

An intensive study of this problem, not only through available literature on college administration and instruction and the factual material resulting from the use of the instruments, but also from extensive personal contact with numerous educational institutions and numerous conferences with college administrative officers, faculty members, and students, has convinced the author that fundamental changes in the administration of higher education are now imperative. Out of this variety of experiences and in the light of the factual material afforded by this study, the author proposes, in this final chapter, a philosophy of college administration which he believes will best provide for adjustment of the college to the changing society of today and its adaptation to the needs of its students.

PHILOSOPHIES OF COLLEGE ADMINISTRATION

The responses of the 330 deans participating in this study reveal that two contrasting theories of administration of higher education appear in the deanship of the liberal arts college. One theory has been called autocratic, the other democratic. In the extreme functioning of the autocratic type, as defined in the in-

[9] Horn, H. H., *The Teacher as Artist*, pp. 46f. (By permission of Houghton Mifflin Company.)

strument of this study, the board of trustees consists of laymen chosen for life by cooptation and clothed with complete authority. This board delegates to the president of its own choosing certain powers and holds him responsible. The president exercises these powers, with the faculty subordinated and student opinion repressed or disregarded. In the extreme democratic type of administration, as defined in the instrument, all control is in the hands of the faculty and students.

Educators who favor the autocratic theory of college administration believe essentially in the monarchic form of government for colleges and in the efficacy of the business pattern of the external lay board. They are committed to the principle of complete centralization of authority. They feel that this system has been successful in the past, and that interference of the faculty or students with the plans of the president or board would lead to administrative and educational inefficiency. This conception has curtly been expressed in these words:

> In the execution of the policy of the institution as determined by the board, he (the president) should have about the same power as the executive officer of a great corporation, but if he be wise he will exercise that power with great caution in the change of officers.[10]

In support of this theory a college president, who signed himself "One of the Guild," wrote in the *Atlantic Monthly*:

> When the directors of a great commercial corporation or some transportation company find it necessary to call a new man to the presidency or position of general manager, he is at once given almost absolute authority as to all executive details. The Board of Control determines the general policy of the company, always after counseling with the new president or manager, and then leaves the executive to carry out this policy. . . . He gathers about him a corps of competent, loyal, ambitious assistants, wisely retaining those whose efficiency is beyond question. . . .
> The educational executive or manager, however, has no such freedom of choice as to his associates. . . . If we are to accomplish even a fair part of all that is easily possible, educationally, in the next century, we must separate quite sharply the work of instruction and the work of administration. . . .
> But the wear and tear and waste and delay must continue almost unbearable, unless the business of education is regarded in a business light, is cared for by business methods, and is made subject to that simple but all-efficient law of a proper division of labor and of intelligent and efficient organization,—a division of labor which brings men who are students of the classics, the sciences, the literature, philosophy, history, under the wise

10 Powers, James K., *College Administration*, p. 5.

direction and immediate control of the man who is necessarily and most desirably a student of humanity, with a responsibility which is coincident with the work in hand, and with an authority entirely commensurate with this responsibility.[11]

Among the arguments stated in behalf of the autocratic conception of college administration are the following:

1. It secures absolute uniformity.[12]

2. It secures a higher grade of talent in administrative positions.[13]

3. It provides for immediate introduction of reforms.[14]

4. It attains maximum efficiency.[15]

5. It secures unity of purpose and coördination in conduct of institution.[16]

6. It does not force executive work upon a non-executive body.[17]

7. It does not violate that principle of government which declares a legislative body should not execute its own legislation.[18]

8. It fixes responsibility.[19]

9. It avoids administrative vacillation and delay.[20]

10. It avoids unwieldiness in administration.[21]

11. It simplifies the machinery of organization.[22]

12. It conserves the time and energy of faculty members and frees them for their primary work.[23]

13. It places affairs upon a business basis and adapts methods of organization and administration which commend themselves to all sane business men in all undertakings.[24]

[11] "One of the Guild." "The Perplexities of a College President," *Atlantic Monthly*, Vol. 85, pp. 485-493, April, 1900.

[12, 13, 14] Thurber, C. H., *The Principles of School Organization*, pp. 14-18.

[15] Thurber, C. H., *op. cit.*, pp. 14-18. Keppel, F. P., *The Undergraduate and His College*, p. 234. Morey, Lloyd, *University and College Accounting*, p. 209. Lindsay, E. E. and Holland, E. O., *College and University Administration*, p. 469.

[16] Kinder, *op. cit.*, p. 61. McVey, F. L., "Administrative Relations in Colleges," *School and Society*, Vol. 28, p. 706, December 8, 1928.

[17] Kinder, *op. cit.*, p. 66. [18] Kinder, *op. cit.*, p. 127.

[19, 20] Reeves, F. W. and Russell, J. D., *College Organization and Administration*, p. 75.

[21] Suzzallo, Henry, "University Organization—What is Best for Educational Efficiency?" *Transactions and Proceedings of the National Association of State Universities*, 1924, p. 91.

[22] Learned, W. S. and Others, *The Professional Preparation of Teachers for American Public Schools*, p. 63.

[23] Suzzallo, *op. cit.*, pp. 90f. Kinder, *op. cit.*, p. 66. Hamilton, F. R., *Fiscal Support of State Teachers Colleges*, p. 21. Klapper, Paul, "The College Teacher and His Professional Status," *Educational Administration and Supervision*, Vol. 11, p. 90, 1925.

[24] "One of the Guild," *loc. cit.*, p. 492.

14. It secures specialization in both administration and teaching.[25]

15. It has succeeded in the past.[26]

Contrasted with this autocratic conception of administration, the extreme democratic theory would place all control in the hands of the faculty and students, as it was in certain older European universities. Among the arguments offered by those who favor some measure of democratic administration in higher education are the following:

1. It stimulates individual initiative.[27]

2. It provides for participation of all interested in the enterprise.[28]

3. It avoids the tendency to substitute mechanism for personality.[29]

4. It avoids dangerous centralization of power—one-man power, which is always objectionable in a university.[30]

5. It does not enfeeble those subject to it nor suppress free inquiry.[31]

6. It does not subordinate educational policy to financial and administrative interests at the expense of the ambitions and hopes of faculties.[32]

7. It does not reduce the place and authority of the teaching group to the level of low estate and influence.[33]

8. It avoids plasticity, conformity and mediocrity in the teaching body.[34]

9. It does not submerge the students and teachers to the goal of "efficiency."[35]

10. It increases self-respect of faculty.[36]

11. It promotes the esprit de corps of the teaching staff.[37]

12. It gives the teacher the necessary social status.[38]

[25] Kinder, op. cit., p. 109. Reeves and Russell, op. cit., p. 75.

[26] Butler, N. M., "University Administration in the United States," Educational Review, Vol. 50, pp. 330, 342, April, 1911.

[27, 28] Thurber, C. H., The Principles of School Organization, pp. 18-22, 29.

[29] Dale, T. N., The Opportunity of the Small College, pp. 4-10.

[30] Kirkpatrick, J. E., Academic Organization and Control, p. 156. Eliot, C. W., University Administration, p. 238.

[31] Cattell, J. McKeen, University Control (quotation from Dr. Seelye), p. 34.

[32] McVey, op. cit., pp. 706, 708.   [33] Ibid., p. 707.   [34] Kirkpatrick, op. cit., p. 155.

[35] Hullfish, H. G. and Thayer, V. T., The Educational Frontier (W. H. Kilpatrick, Editor), p. 209.

[36] McVey, op. cit., p. 709. Ruthven, A. G., "University Organization," School and Society, Vol. 31, p. 746, May 31, 1930.

[37] Thwing, C. F., The American College, p. 51.   [38] Kirkpatrick, op. cit., p. 156.

13. It develops self-reliance in teachers.[39]
14. It gives dignity, honor and freedom to the professorial office and stimulates great contributions on the part of the competent faculty members.[40]
15. It stimulates the interest of the faculty.[41]
16. It enlists the interest of the faculty in problems of the institution and preserves the democratic tone.[42]
17. It secures coöperation, proportion and efficiency.[43]
18. It utilizes the wisdom of many which is better than the wisdom of one.[44]
19. It is sympathetic to the freedom of the teacher and is American.[45]
20. It is more apt to secure progress.[46]
21. It secures the worthwhile benefits of student participation.[47]
22. It secures better teachers because of its wider freedom and enlarged opportunity for initiative.[48]
23. It makes for democracy, freedom and intelligence.[49]
24. It harmonizes the government of a university with the ideal of an intellectual organization.[50]

Of the 330 deans participating in this study, a very few marked themselves at either extreme end of the democratic-autocratic self-rating scale. The great majority of the group, and the group as a whole, classified themselves on the democratic side of the scale. The adjusted mean for the group was 70, representing a position 70% toward the democratic end of the self-rating scale.

With this position, indicated by the group as a whole, the author is in general agreement. It contemplates as much democracy in

[39] Hylla, Erich; quoted in *Academic Organization and Control* (Kirkpatrick, J. E., author), p. 149.
[40] Cattell, *op. cit.*, p. 7.
[41] McVey, *op. cit.*, p. 709. Eells, W. C., *The Junior College*, p. 383. McConn, Max, *College or Kindergarten*, p. 260. Quigley, H. S., "Faculty-Administration Relations in a College of Liberal Arts," *School and Society*, Vol. 36, p. 268, August 27, 1932.
[42] Klein, A. J., *Survey of Rutgers University*, p. 103.
[43] Thwing, *op. cit.*, p. 51. Ladd, G. T., "The Need of Administrative Changes in the University," *University Control* (J. McKeen Cattell, Ed.), p. 368. Munroe, J. P. "Closer Relations Between Trustees and Faculty," *University Control* (J. McKeen Cattell, Ed.), p. 473.
[44] Thwing, *op. cit.*, p. 51.
[45] Kelly, R. L., *Tendencies in College Administration*, p. 27.
[46] McVey, *op. cit.*, p. 709.
[47] Richardson, L. B., A *Study of the Liberal Arts College*, p. 278.
[48] Thwing, *op. cit.*, pp. 49ff. Cattell, *op. cit.*, p. 18.
[49] Kirkpatrick, *op. cit.*, pp. 156f.
[50] Schurman, J. G., "Faculty Participation in University Government," *University Control* (J. McKeen Cattell, Ed.), p. 476.

college administration as seems consistent with the efficient functioning of the institution. Unity of purpose, democratic spirit, and coöperation are the conditions that should obtain in institutions of higher learning.

By a reliable percentage vote this group of deans expressed its belief that "the purpose of a college can best be realized by placing the responsibility for internal administration in the hands of the administrators and faculty in coöperation." The author shares the same belief. In reference to this highly controversial issue, Arthur J. Klein has aptly written:

The principle of university administration which maintains that good organization and management will free as large a proportion of the faculty as possible from administrative duties and make such work for those who must participate as light as necessities permit in order that the faculty may devote itself to teaching, research, and intellectual growth, is in constant conflict with the equally valid principle that the interest of the faculty must be enlisted in the problems of the institution and that a démocratic tone must be maintained in the educational administration of our higher institutions by faculty participation in the activities and responsibilities of management. Administrative wisdom no doubt will recognize both principles and carry neither to an extreme.[61]

The term "administrative wisdom," with its implication in the foregoing statement, well expresses a major qualification of a dean or president. The emphasis with which the group of deans included in this study favors the democratic conception of administration, as well as their reliable percentage votes on a number of statements, indicates that college administrators are not nearly so autocratic as the mechanism they administer would suggest. The strong probability is that college administration is much more democratic in practice than it is in form, and that deans, generally, administer their trusts with common sense and in a spirit of consideration for others.

Democracy in college administration that involves both faculty and students, as favored by this group of deans, is in line with what the author believes the best educational thought of the time. In the final analysis, the real college consists of the teachers and students. Its paramount functions are teaching and learning. Its primary duty is to develop the abilities of faculty and students. Administration is but a means to that end. Its sole reason for existence is to facilitate this development. The type of administra-

[61] Klein, Arthur J., *Survey of Rutgers University*, p. 103.

tion that best achieves this development must be judged the proper one. The type that denies this fullest development must be condemned as harmful. In this connection Dr. George D. Strayer suggests a pertinent criterion:

> The one most important criterion by which to judge of the work of the administrator is found in the query: "Have those who have been associated with him grown?" It is not to be expected that all will have achieved great distinction, but the demand may well be made that all do better work and that all are ready to accept greater responsibility.[52]

Dr. Hullfish and Dr. Thayer have recently written:

> Administrative concerns that submerge both student and teacher and elevate the goal of "efficiency" will not be tolerated.[53]

In regard to "efficiency" Professor W. H. Kilpatrick has written:

> The efficiency of a school system lies of course primarily in its social-educative effects. To this all else is subordinate. Business efficiency is, to be sure, necessary in all matters pertaining to expending of money, but the ultimate question is as to how well the social-educative aims of the system are fostered and similarly with the management of teachers and accounting of pupils. Success is ultimately to be judged by the social-educative results, to the teachers themselves, to the pupils, to the community.[54]

Dr. John Dewey has touched pertinently upon this point:

> The control afforded by the customs and regulations of others may be short-sighted. It may accomplish its immediate effect, but at the expense of throwing the subsequent action of the person out of balance.[55]

The business pattern has become almost an idol in American life. The apparent success of this administrative pattern in industry convinced many educators and boards of trustees that it could be applied with equal success in the realm of higher education. Such a conclusion seemed valid on the surface, but it failed to take into consideration the fact that many factors existed in the educational situation that were not present in the business enterprise. Its success in business, therefore, did not guarantee its success as an administrative pattern for colleges and universities. Buildings and endowments, and even rapid formulation and execution of policies, are not the real test of the efficiency of a college. That

[52] Strayer, George D., "Creative Administration," *Teachers College Record*, Vol. 27, p. 4, September 1925.
[53] Kilpatrick, W. H. (Editor), *The Educational Frontier*, p. 209.
[54] *Ibid.*, pp. 283f.
[55] Dewey, John, *Democracy and Education*, p. 31.

test most certainly lies in the rounded development of faculty and students, in the "social-educative values" that have accrued from the work of the institution.

In the light of this philosophy, with which this group of deans seems in general agreement, administration in higher education cannot justifiably disregard the faculty nor repress the student body. Considering the degree of maturity of the student, he must be recognized as a valid force and his judgments given proper consideration. A mere semblance of student participation is but sheer hypocrisy. From their experiments in student participation at Colorado State Teachers College, President Frasier and Principal Wrinkle concluded:

Student government thrives best under a strong, actively-interested college administration and makes least progress under a passive institutional attitude. . . . Colleges should spend time and energy in developing the right kind of student participation in government.[56]

Professor L. B. Richardson, of Dartmouth, after studying the results of student participation at the University of Chicago, Purdue University, Princeton University, Bowdoin College, Dartmouth College, and other institutions, summed up his general findings as follows:

. . . it seems to be a fair conclusion that wherever student participation has been intelligently applied, the benefits are real and well worth the effort.[57]

The group of deans included in this study indicated, by a reliable percentage, their belief that the chief value of student criticism lay in the fact that, in the determination of college policies, the student's point of view formed a good supplement to the faculty point of view. To ascertain, regularly and adequately, this student viewpoint with the intention of utilizing its value requires an active institutional attitude in favor of student participation and satisfactory provision for the expression of student opinion.

This group of deans likewise indicated, by a reliable percentage vote, that the purpose of the college can best be realized by placing the responsibility for internal administration in the hands of the administrators and faculty in coöperation. In the functioning of this type of administration the faculty would be more than the legislative body of the institution. It would develop, recommend,

[56] Frasier, Wrinkle, and Others, *An Experiment in Student Participation*, pp. 53, 59.
[57] Richardson, L. B., *A Study of the Liberal Arts College*, p. 278.

and assist in the execution of the educational policies of the college. It is assumed that the participation of faculty members in administration would be within properly circumscribed spheres and that they would bear full responsibility to the extent of their participation. As announced recently by President Ruthven, in his last annual report, the University of Michigan is rapidly developing this type of internal administration, a movement that is shared by a number of other institutions of higher learning.

It is the author's belief that an internal administration of this type, as favored by the deans participating in this study, democratic and coöperative, in the hands of competent men, would go far toward creating a college of unified purpose, maximum efficiency, and genial atmosphere, where faculty, students, and administrators alike would be imbued with enthusiasm and eagerness to learn from one another as they studied together the problems of higher education.

AGREEMENT OF DEANS ON CERTAIN COLLEGE PROBLEM SOLUTIONS

The philosophy of administration described above finds particular application in this study to the office of dean and to the solution of certain controversial issues in higher education. It is clearly revealed in the great majority of the forty-three statements and alternatives that drew reliable percentage votes and particularly in the numerous democratic responses that found favor in the judgments of the deans. The consensus of opinion of the group of deans participating in this study was that the purpose of the college definitely needs clarification at this time. In this conclusion the author heartily concurs. Professor B. H. Bode, of Ohio State University, has pertinently written, in connection with this problem:

In view of this development, it is no wonder that there has been increasing dissatisfaction with the college of liberal arts. Its original unity of purpose has been completely lost. This fact can scarcely be disguised by vague talk about the breadth or background to be obtained from a college education. The vaunted breadth is not so much breadth as a confusion of breadth with variety. We have incorporated a number of diverse values into the curriculum by a process of compartmentalization. We teach a little of everything and then we apparently expect the students to achieve out of the total mass of their learnings a synthesis which, up to the present, the college has been quite unable to achieve for itself. . . .

In brief, the basic trouble with the modern college is that, like Stephen

Leacock's horseman, it rides off in all directions at once. . . . The accumulation of credits may qualify a student for graduation; it does not qualify
him for intelligent living. . . .

In a word, college education should be concerned primarily with the
task of assisting every student to develop an independent philosophy of
life.[58]

In the clarification of the purpose of the college, the dean of
the faculty should play a responsible part. Reform in college education must come about largely through the influence of college
administrative and professional forces, as the deans have indicated.
That the liberal arts college, generally, has lagged behind the recent development in social and economic needs, there seems little
doubt. To adapt the purpose of the college to the present needs of
students is a policy that should immediately be put into execution.
This policy, indicated by the vote of the deans and confirmed by
extensive study, would recognize that equality of opportunity to
secure a suitable education should obtain in higher education; that
before admission of a student the college should have all possible
cumulative information about him that is pertinent to his college
career; that the values of Freshman Week and Orientation
Courses should be made available to him; that there should be provision in the curriculum for the mediocre student as well as for the
average and superior; that there should be constant revision of
the curriculum, under the active guidance of the dean; that the
college should endeavor to foster experiences for the rounded development of its students; that it should present, through its curriculum and instruction, all social and economic doctrines; that an
organization with a few (four or five) major divisions is probably
more effective in securing the aims of liberal education; that student rating of instructors has some value; that the instructor
should have knowledge of his own rating by his students; that
personality and teaching ability are prime essentials in the qualifications of an effective college instructor; that either individualized or group teaching, as determined by conditions and subjects,
may be the best type of instruction at the college level; that for the
evaluation of teaching methods experimentation should be made
to determine the proper criteria; that both subjective and objective type tests, in some rational proportion, should be used in examinations in courses; that the present system of qualification for

[58] Bode, B. H., "Aims in College Teaching," *Journal of Higher Education*, Vol. III,
No. 9, pp. 478f, December, 1932.

graduation by an accumulation of credits and quality grade points should be supplemented by comprehensive examinations in the student's major field in the senior year; that instruction may be improved by more frequent contact between student and instructor; that vocational guidance of its students and placement and follow-up of its graduates are proper responsibilities of the liberal arts college.

REORGANIZATION OF OFFICE OF DEAN

Elsewhere in this study have been pointed out many glaring defects in the organization and administration of the deanship. During the course of this investigation numerous letters have been received from deans of liberal arts colleges inquiring if, as a result of this study, a definition of the duties and prerogatives of a dean had been developed with sufficient completeness to make it a standard to be followed. That these duties should be adequately defined, there can be little doubt.

In their "Survey of Higher Education for the United Lutheran Church in America," made in 1929, Leonard, Evenden and O'Rear stated an essential principle of college administration in these words:

An adequate staff can work efficiently only if the duties of each have been clearly defined.[59]

This principle has been grossly violated by many liberal arts colleges. Kinder reports, in a study only recently published, that in 55% of the 90 liberal arts colleges reporting on this item in his survey no definition of the duties of the several offices had been made.[60]

It would seem that the first logical step toward improvement of the deanship is a clear definition of the duties and responsibilities of the office. Such a definition should be made by each institution for its own deanship. This procedure would offer sufficient latitude for desirable variation and at the same time preclude excessive standardization of the office. It is generally agreed that while a certain amount of standardization would promote improvement in the functioning of the office, a high degree of standardization might nullify all the benefits thus derived. There are local colorings of the situation and personality traits of the incumbent that

[59] Leonard, Evenden, O'Rear, and Others, *op. cit.*, p. 6.
[60] Kinder, *op. cit.*, pp. 45f.

may justifiably require variation in duties. Beyond this desirable variation there is doubtless a core of duties common to the office and logically belonging to it, in a large number of institutions. These duties might well form the nucleus for general organization of the functions of the deanship.

As the situation exists today, the variation, not the standardization, is excessive. The fact that the dean, in one or another of 116 colleges and universities, is performing all 60 functions listed for all the administrative offices combined (see page 27), supports the belief that a certain measure of standardization is requisite for the proper organization of the office. The deanship is now generally accepted as an essential administrative office in higher educational institutions. As such, its major duties and responsibilities should be clearly understood.

The definition of these major duties and responsibilities should be made with the conception in mind of the dean as a leader in the field of higher education. In all too many institutions today, particularly those of smaller enrollments, the dean is burdened by a multiplicity of small duties. Toothman found that 81.27% of the time of the dean, in the average situation, is devoted to ten functions which deal almost wholly with routine matters.[61] Many of these minor duties may properly be assigned to subordinate officers or clerical assistants, thereby freeing the dean for assumption of more important responsibilities. It is not proposed that he be relieved of all teaching duties, nor is it probable that this group of deans would concur in such a recommendation. Such action is obviously impracticable at this time, save in the larger institutions. But the teaching load of the dean should be radically reduced. An average teaching load that consumes 36.42% of his time,[62] and, in a group of smaller colleges, extends beyond sixteen hours (see page 26), is obviously excessive. It is well for the dean to do some teaching, where the conditions permit, but his time must be safeguarded to the extent that his major responsibilities do not suffer in the process.

The major responsibilities of the dean depend very largely upon the place the deanship occupies in the total administrative organization of the college. It is necessary, therefore, to determine, in a simple, convenient fashion, the broad areas of service of the several administrative officers of the institution who occupy major

[61] Toothman, *op. cit.*, p. 239.   [62] Toothman, *op. cit.*, p. 237.

executive positions. The number of these officers and the degree of their specialization increase as institutions of larger enrollments are taken into consideration. The university, with its several major divisions, presents a complex situation which cannot be so simply outlined. But the independent liberal arts college, which was most widely represented in this study, does readily yield to a convenient division of administrative organization. It is, therefore, possible to state, in general terms, the relationships between the office of dean and the other major administrative offices usually found in the independent liberal arts college.

The president of the college heads the executive unit of administration. As chief executive officer, he has general oversight over the work of all other offices of administration. Particularly is he the liaison officer between the constituency, the board, and the college. He represents the institution in its relations to students, alumni, parents, and the general public. He sees that a prográm is developed through which the institution may render appropriate service.

The dean of the faculty heads the instructional unit of internal administration. His responsibilities are primarily in relation to the faculty and students. He has general charge of the educational guidance of the students and is concerned with the internal problems of the teaching staff.

The business and finance unit of the institution is immediately managed by such officers as business manager, bursar, comptroller, treasurer, financial secretary, etc., who are directly responsible to the president.

The publicity and public relations unit, manned by public relations officers, is likewise generally directed by the president.

MAJOR RESPONSIBILITIES OF DEANSHIP

The major responsibilities of the dean may be said to lie within the following areas: (1) instruction, (2) curriculum, (3) student welfare, (4) personnel, (5) faculty relations, (6) admissions, (7) discipline, (8) research. He has, of course, additional responsibilities for which he does not assume the major rôle. Among these are the budget and public relations. It is his duty to guide the budget through the several departments, but there are sections of the budget with which he is not concerned, such as appropriations for the business offices, power plant, and the like. Also, he is under some obligation to interpret the institution to society and should give some time and thought to public relations, but the public relations unit itself should be under the general direction of the president.

The dean of the faculty is primarily charged with responsibility for the administration of the instructional program of the college. In a democratic and coöperative spirit he should supervise the curricula and courses of study; initiate and actively guide curriculum revision; supervise the making of schedules; develop, with the assistance of the faculty, a program for the improvement of instruction.

The dean has a particular responsibility to the students, for their welfare, adjustments, and educational guidance. To secure effective coördination in the interest of the student, the personnel records may well be centralized in the office of the dean, and the personnel work proceed under his general direction.

In many of the larger institutions separate personnel units have developed, operating under the direction of the president. It is urged by those who favor this type of organization that it affords less overlapping, greater efficiency and economy, better unification and coöperation, less confusion and conflict, more complete personnel service to the student, and definitely fixes responsibility for personnel work. They propose, therefore, a separate division of university administration to be known as Student Personnel. Such a division has been in existence at Northwestern University since 1922, and has been duplicated in other large institutions. The chief objection to this type of organization lies in the fact that it tends to divorce personnel work from other student welfare activities, thus defeating coördination in the interest of the student. More recently, therefore, among larger institutions there has been discerned a distinct tendency to establish an inclusive office, such as dean of students, which would thoroughly integrate all student welfare and personnel work into a single effective centralized organization. Illustrations of this development are to be found at the University of Oregon, University of Pennsylvania, University of Chicago, and Purdue University.

But so far as the independent college of liberal arts, with a single-type organization, is concerned, unified control of student records and coördination of personnel activities seem most readily attainable through centralization in the office of the dean. Such was the recommendation of the Committee on Educational Counseling and Administration, of the American College Personnel Association, as reported at Minneapolis in February, 1933.

> The administration of educational counseling depends almost entirely on the size and organization of the individual institution. In the smaller college offering but one type of training such as the liberal arts college, experience seems to indicate that it is most advantageous to have the personnel program headed by the Academic Dean. In large institutions other set-ups have proved more efficient, the program being headed by an administrative officer or a committee of the faculty.[63]

Such an organization does, indeed, seem logical, since the dean is himself a personnel officer, with definite personnel relations to both faculty and students. He is definitely responsible for the educational guidance of the students, and this entails the use of personnel records and the information which they contain. Furthermore, the interest and sympathy of the dean in personnel problems seem definitely essential if any real measure of success is to attend endeavors in this field. Under his aggressive leadership personnel specialists should find ever-widening opportunities for the development of their work and students should benefit increasingly. Should a group of teaching faculty members adapted to advisory work or deans of men and women, with faculty assistants, carry on the personnel work, as the deans in this study seem to prefer, the organization here suggested is likewise logical and desirable.

As dean of the faculty, all faculty problems properly lie within his jurisdiction. He is the natural representative of the faculty in its relations to the president and often in its relations to the public. He recommends appointments and promotions, harmonizes conflicting interests, assists in the solution of departmental and individual problems.

The dean should, through the registrar, oversee the admissions system, but should not actually evaluate credits. He likewise should keep in touch with discipline, which should be handled directly by the offices of dean of men and dean of women, or, in their absence, by other properly constituted agencies.

The dean should supervise the research program of the institution, as determined by the faculty, and the work of the research

[63] Committee on Educational Counseling and Administration of American College Personnel Association (Miss Helen MacM. Voorhees, Chairman), *Tenth Annual Report of the American College Personnel Association,* 1933, p. 30.

specialists on the staff. Whether this research program should involve public projects for the community or be limited to the requirements of the college is a problem for the institution itself to decide. It seems both feasible and advisable, however, for each institution to set up a research committee from its faculty for the study of its own problems. Student adjustments, curriculum revision, improvement of instruction are fertile fields for research within each institution, and in these problems the dean has a vital interest.

SELECTION OF DEANS

The adequate performance of these major functions, briefly listed above, requires an educational engineer of high order. Upon what basis is it reasonable to expect such a leader can be secured? Not on the basis of seniority, nor long service, nor advancing age, nor light teaching load. The employment of such criteria must certainly, in all too many instances, bring inefficiency to administration and disaster to faculty and students. Perhaps it was some such situation as this that called forth this scathing indictment from Dr. C. C. Little:

> The degree to which overtaxed deans can misunderstand and bully youth is almost unbelievable to those who have not come in contact with it. . . . The dean has permanency of tenure. Nothing but battle, murder or sudden death can dislodge him. . . . There is need of a house cleaning and of a recognition of new and more human values. . . .
>
> Once or twice in a generation a great humanitarian like former Dean Briggs of Harvard lights up the lives and hearts of hundreds of students, but his appearance is a miracle, a kindness of nature, and not to be called forth by the routine methods or plans of men. It is safer and saner to try to develop a "fool proof" method, producing a less miraculous but more certain solution of the problem. It is wiser to bring the abstract qualities of understanding, love of youth, and sympathy in to our colleges as recognized principles; and to engrave them there by the establishment of a strong group of officers pledged to mutual cooperation and to common ideals in their perpetuation.[64]

In the phrase "routine methods or plans of men" Dr. Little has placed his finger pertinently upon the source of much present-day difficulty in regard to the deanship. It is appropriate to recall in this connection that Dean Briggs, the "great humanitarian," was not selected by "routine methods." It was not seniority that won him the appointment, for many of his colleagues exceeded him in

[64] Little, Clarence C., *The Awakening College*, pp. 66f.

this respect. Nor was light teaching load the occasion for his promotion. His courses were outstandingly popular and he carried one of the heaviest teaching loads in the university. Neither was it length of service that won him the appointment, for in 1891, the year of his selection as Dean of the College, he had been a teacher of English at Harvard just eight years. Finally, it was not age that dictated his promotion, for he was thirty-five when made Dean of the College and forty-six when made Dean of the Faculty of Arts and Sciences.

President Eliot was severely criticized because he "appointed a mere boy to the chief disciplinary position of the university." By this act "he incurred the displeasure of some members of the faculty and a few members of the governing boards."[65] Most members of the faculty, including George Herbert Palmer, believed the appointment unwise. Thirty-five years later, however, Professor Palmer made this statement:

I believed then, as I still believe, that President Eliot possessed more of the elements of greatness than any man I had ever known; and I had the utmost confidence in his judgment of men. But when he appointed Briggs to the deanship, it seemed to me nothing short of an absolute joke. Briggs had been in my classes, and I had found him a delightful man and a capital student. But how could this pink-faced boy, so shrinking that he could scarcely stand before men and express himself coherently, ever be expected to perform police duty for the college? He had not been appointed long, however, before I discovered that we were no longer on the police basis. He soon became the best Dean the college ever had.[66]

What criteria, then, did President Eliot employ in deciding to appoint Professor Briggs to the deanship? His own words, spoken many years later, were:

My information about him was more complete than anyone supposed. I had known his father and his mother; so I was sure his inheritance was sound. I had seen the man himself develop in a few years from a modest tutor to one of the able teachers of the university. I had discovered that he possessed a high honesty, a readiness to give himself to others, and a certain charming kindliness of character which made men at ease in his presence and encouraged them to be confidential with him. Of course, there was also a personal ground: I liked the man and I was ready to believe that the feeling was not all on one side. I feel sure, however, that my chief reason for appointing him was this: I had discovered that students were going to him for counsel on every kind of problem, and I thought they might keep on going to him, even if he was Dean.[67]

[65] Brown, Rollo Walter, *Dean Briggs*, pp. 96ff. (By permission of Harper &. Brothers.)
[66] *Ibid.*, pp. 97f.   [67] *Ibid.*, pp. 96f.

In the selection of Dean Briggs it is evident that the great Harvard president threw "routine" to the winds and made his choice on the basis of genuine qualifications for the office.

The only basis upon which genuine leadership can be secured in the deanship is a combination of three qualifications: (1) scholarship, (2) professional training and experience, and (3) natural endowment of mind and heart.

In the reorganized deanship, as revealed by the emerging conception, the successful incumbent will be a man of ripe scholarship, broad professional training, thorough familiarity with the problems of higher education, intellectual enough to command the respect of faculties and human enough to win and hold the confidence of students.

SUMMARY

This chapter describes an emerging conception of the deanship, as indicated by the data presented in this study. This conception contemplates the office so organized as to include the major responsibilities that seem natural to an efficient, democratic administration, and staffed by an educational leader who is scholarly, trained, experienced, human, and dominated by a democratic philosophy of administration.

Bibliography

BOOKS

ADAMS, H. B. *Thomas Jefferson and the University of Virginia.* United States Government Printing Office, Washington, D. C., 1888.

BODE, B. H. *Fundamentals of Education.* The Macmillan Company, New York, 1928.

BODE, B. H. *Modern Educational Theories.* The Macmillan Company, New York, 1927.

BRONSON, W. C. *The History of Brown University (1764–1914).* Brown University Press, Providence, R. I., 1914.

BROOKS, R. C. *Reading for Honors at Swarthmore.* Oxford University Press, New York, 1927.

BROWN, R. W. *Dean Briggs.* Harper & Brothers, New York, 1926.

CLARK, T. A. *Discipline and the Derelict.* The Macmillan Company, New York, 1922.

COLLINS, V. L. *Princeton.* Oxford University Press, New York, 1914.

COLLIER, C. B. *The Dean of the State Teachers College.* Peabody Contributions to Education No. 24. George Peabody College for Teachers, Nashville, Tenn., 1926.

COPE, A. *History of Ohio State University.* Columbus, Ohio, 1920.

COTTRELL, D. P. *Instruction and Instructional Facilities in the Colleges of the United Lutheran Church in America.* Contributions to Education, No. 376. Bureau of Publications, Teachers College, Columbia University, New York, 1929.

COUNTS, G. S. *The American Road to Culture.* The John Day Company, New York, 1930.

DEMAREST, W. H. S. *History of Rutgers College (1766–1924).* Rutgers University Press, New Brunswick, N. J., 1924.

DEWEY, J. *Democracy and Education.* The Macmillan Company, New York, 1926.

DEWEY, J. *Experience and Nature.* Open Court Publishing Company, Chicago, 1929.

EATON, T. H. *College Teaching.* John Wiley & Sons, Inc., New York, 1932.

ELIOT, C. W. *University Administration.* Houghton Mifflin Company, Boston, 1908.

EVENDEN, E. S. "Predicted Changes in the Curriculum of Teachers Colleges by 1950." *Eighth Yearbook of the American Association of Teachers Colleges,* 1929.

FRASIER, G. W. AND OTHERS. *Experiments in Teachers College Administration.* Warwick & York, Inc., Baltimore, 1929.

FREELAND, G. E. *The Improvement of Teaching.* The Macmillan Company, New York, 1924.

FULTON, M. G. (Editor). *College Life, Its Conditions and Problems.* The Macmillan Company, New York, 1920.

FITZPATRICK, E. A. *St. Ignatius and the Ratio Studiorum.* McGraw-Hill Book Company, Inc., New York, 1933.

GARDINER, J. H. *Harvard.* Oxford University Press, New York, 1914.

GOOD, C. V. *Teaching in College and University.* Warwick & York, Inc., Baltimore, 1929.

HARPER, M. H. *Social Beliefs and Attitudes of American Educators.* Contributions to Education, No. 294. Bureau of Publications, Teachers College, Columbia University, New York, 1927.

HAWKES, H. E. *College—What's the Use?* Doubleday, Page and Company, New York, 1927.

HITCHCOCK, E. *Reminiscences of Amherst College.* Bridgman and Childs, Northampton, Mass., 1863.

HUDELSON, E. AND OTHERS. *Problems of College Education.* University of Minnesota, Minneapolis, 1928.

JAMES, E. J. *Sixteen Years at the University of Illinois.* University of Illinois Press, Urbana, Ill., 1920.

JOHNSON, M. N. *The Dean in the High School.* Professional and Technical Press, New York, 1929.

JONES, J. L. *A Personnel Study of Women Deans in Colleges and Universities.* Contributions to Education No. 326. Bureau of Publications, Teachers College, Columbia University, 1928.

KELLY, F. J. *The American Arts College.* The Macmillan Company, New York, 1925.

KELLY, R. L. AND OTHERS. *The Effective College.* Association of American Colleges, New York, 1928.

KENT, R. A. AND OTHERS. *Higher Education in America.* Ginn and Company, Boston, 1930.

KEPPEL, F. P. *Columbia.* Oxford University Press, New York, 1914.

KEPPEL, F. P. *The Undergraduate and His College.* Houghton Mifflin Company, Boston, 1917.

KILPATRICK, W. H. AND OTHERS. *The Educational Frontier.* The Century Company, New York, 1933.

KINDER, J. C. *The Internal Administration of the Liberal Arts College.* Contributions to Education No. 597. Bureau of Publications, Teachers College, Columbia University, New York, 1934.

LEONARD, R. J., EVENDEN, E. S., AND O'REAR, F. B. *Survey of Higher Education for the United Lutheran Church in America.* Bureau of Publications, Teachers College, Columbia University, New York, 1929.

LINDSAY, E. E. AND HOLLAND, E. O. *College and University Administration.* The Macmillan Company, New York, 1930.

LITTLE, C. C. *The Awakening College.* W. W. Norton & Company, Inc., New York, 1930.

LORD, J. K. *A History of Dartmouth College.* The Rumford Press, Concord, N. H., 1913.

LUBBERS, I. J. *College Organization and Administration.* Northwestern University Press, Evanston, Ill., 1932.

MATTHEWS, B. (Editor). *A History of Columbia University (1754–1904).* The Macmillan Company, New York, 1904.

McGUCKEN, S. J. *The Jesuits and Education.* The Bruce Publishing Company, Milwaukee, 1932.

MENDENHALL, T. C. *History of Ohio State University.* Ohio State University Press, Columbus, 1926.

MERRILL, R. A. AND BRAGDON, H. D. *The Vocation of Dean.* Press and Publicity Committee, National Association of Deans of Women, New York, 1926.

MORRISON, R. H. *Internal Administrative Organization in Teachers Colleges.* Contributions to Education, No. 592. Bureau of Publications, Teachers College, Columbia University, New York, 1933.

PIERCE, A. E. *Deans and Advisers of Women and Girls.* Professional and Technical Press, New York, 1928.

RAUP, R. B. *Problems in Philosophy of Education.* Teachers College Syllabi, No. 14. Bureau of Publications, Teachers College, Columbia University, New York, 1927.

REEVES, F. W. AND RUSSELL, J. D. *College Organization and Administration.* Board of Education, Disciples of Christ, Indianapolis, 1929.

REEVES, F. W. AND RUSSELL, J. D. *The Liberal Arts College.* Board of Education, Methodist Episcopal Church, Chicago, 1932.

RICHARDSON, L. B. *History of Dartmouth College.* Hanover, N. H., 1932.

SLOSSON, E. E. *Great American Universities.* The Macmillan Company, New York, 1910.

SNEDDEN, D. *What's Wrong with American Education?* J. B. Lippincott Company, New York, 1927.

STURTEVANT, S. M. AND STRANG, R. *A Personnel Study of the Deans of Women in Teachers Colleges and Normal Schools.* Contributions to Education No. 319. Bureau of Publications, Teachers College, Columbia University, New York, 1928.

Survey of Land-Grant Colleges and Universities. United States Office of Education, Washington, D. C., 1930.

The Americana. Americana Corporation, New York, 1932.

TAYLOR, J. M. AND HAIGHT, E. H. *Vassar.* Oxford University Press, New York, 1915.

THWING, C. F. *The American and German Universities.* The Macmillan Company, New York, 1928.

TOOTHMAN, H. F. *The Academic Dean of the Liberal Arts College.* Unpublished dissertation, University of Cincinnati, Cincinnati, 1933.

VAN AMRINGE, J. H. *Historical Sketch of Columbia College in the City of New York (1754–1876).* Columbia College Press, New York, 1876.

MAGAZINES, PERIODICALS, AND BULLETINS

ADAMS, SIR JOHN. "Integralism." *Higher Education Faces the Future.* (Edited by P. A. Schilpp). Horace Liveright, New York, 1930.

BODE, B. H. "Aims in College Teaching." *Journal of Higher Education,* Vol. III, pp. 475-480, December, 1932.

BOUCHER, C. S. "The New Plan of the University of Chicago." *Recent Trends in American College Education.* (W. S. Gray, Editor). University of Chicago Press, Chicago, 1931.

CARPENTER, W. W. AND CARTER, W. R. "Duties of the Dean of the Public Junior College." *Peabody Journal of Education,* Vol. VII, pp. 218-223, January, 1930.

CLARK, T. A. "History and Development of the Office of Dean of Men." *School and Society,* Vol. XVI, pp. 65-70, July 15, 1922.

COTTRELL, D. P. "The Measurement of Conflicting Viewpoints in Higher Education." *Teachers College Record,* Vol. XXXIV, pp. 635-654, May, 1933.

DEWEY, J. "The Goal of Education." *The New York Times,* Nov. 1, 1931.

Encyclopedia Britannica, 14th Edition, 1929.

FRANK, G. "The Issues of the Day." *The New York Times,* June 28, 1931.

FRILEY, C. E. "The Place of the Dean in the Administrative Organization of the College." *Bulletin, Agricultural and Mechanical College of Texas,* June 1, 1928.

GOOD, C. V. "Administration and Supervision of Students by Advisers in a Teacher-Training Institution." *Educational Administration and Supervision,* Vol. XII, pp. 161-169, March 1926.

GOOD, C. V. "Methods in Teacher Training." *Journal of Higher Education,* Vol. I, p. 458, November 1930.

GREEN, R. E. "Administrative Dean of the Public Junior College." *School Executives Magazine,* Vol. 49, pp. 122-124, November 1929.

GREENOUGH, C. H. "The Student Council and the Dean at Harvard." *School and Society,* Vol. XXVII, pp. 527-529, May 5, 1928.

HAWKES, H. E. "College Administration." *Journal of Higher Education,* Vol. I, pp. 245-253, May, 1930.

HAWKES, H. E. "Dean to Dean." *Proceedings of the National Education Association,* 1926, pp. 447-453.

HAZZARD, J. C. "The Duties of a Dean of a Small College." *Teachers Journal and Abstract,* Vol. 2, pp. 213-214, March 1927.

HILL, CLYDE M. "Mark Hopkins on a Log." *School and Society,* Vol. XXXV, p. 719, May 28, 1932.

HOFFMAN, B. R. "Correlation of the Work of High School and College Deans." *North Carolina Teacher,* Vol. IV, pp. 122-127, February 1928.

KELLY, R. L. "The Minnesota Colleges, Their Contribution to Society." *Bulletin of Association of American Colleges,* Vol. XIV, pp. 247-306, May 1928.

KEPPEL, F. P. "Administrative Organization of the University." *Educational Review,* Vol. XL, October 1910.

KEPPEL, F. P. "College and University Administration." *Proceedings of the National Education Association,* 1910, pp. 542-547.

KNIGHT, E. W. "Consider the Deans, How They Toil." *School and Society,* Vol. 27, pp. 649-653, June 2, 1928.

MELBY, E. O. AND LIEN, A. "A Practical Technique for Determining the Relative Effectiveness of Different Methods of Teaching." *Journal of Educational Research*, Vol. XIX, pp. 255-264, April, 1929.

MILNER, C. A. "Some Functions of a College Dean." *Bulletin of the Association of American Colleges*, Vol. XVII, pp. 518-521, December 1931.

PEARCE, E. M. "The Dean's Work One of High Status Among Professions." *North Dakota Teacher*, Vol. VII, pp. 13-14, May 1928.

"Report of Committee U." *Proceedings of American Association of University Professors*, Vol. XVIII, December, 1932.

RICHARDS, FLORENCE L. "Deans." *Proceedings of the National Education Association*, 1918, pp. 399-402.

SEASHORE, CARL E. "The Dean's Office." *Trends in Graduate Work, University of Iowa (Fifty Years of Progress)*, 1925.

STONE, H. E. "The University Dean of Men." *School and Society*, Vol. 28, pp. 347-350, September 22, 1928.

STRANG, R. "A Method of Gathering Information about the Profession of Dean of Women." *Vocational Guidance Magazine*, Vol. VII, pp. 105-114, December 1928.

STRANG, R. "Who Performs Personnel Duties?" *School Review*, Vol. XXIX, pp. 33-41, January, 1931.

STURTEVANT, S. M. "What Is a Professional Course for Deans of Women." *School and Society*, Vol. XXIX, pp. 259-262, September 1, 1928.

STURTEVANT, S. M. AND HAYES, H. "A Partial Bibliography for Deans of Women and Girls." *Teachers College Record*, Vol. XXIX, pp. 28-47, April, 1928.

STURTEVANT, S. M. AND OTHERS. "Turnover Among Deans of Women." *Personnel Research*, Vol. VIII, pp. 384-392, April 1930.

THURBER, C. H. "Deans." *The Nation*, November 13, 1913.

THWING, C. F. "College Presidents, Whence Do They Come, Whither Do They Go, What Do They Do?" *School and Society*, Vol. XXXV, pp. 1-8, January 2, 1932.

UNITED STATES OFFICE OF EDUCATION. *Educational Directory, Part III, Colleges and Universities.* Bulletin, 1933, No. 1, 73-111.

WOOLLEY, MARY M. "Deans." *Proceedings of the National Education Association*, 1918, pp. 411-413.

ZOOK, G. F. "The Administration of Personnel Work." *Journal of Higher Education*, Vol. III, pp. 349-354, October, 1932.

Appendix A

LIST OF COOPERATING COLLEGES

Legend: (1) Historical questionnaire omitted. (2) Instrument omitted. (3) "Test on Controversial Issues" omitted.

ALABAMA

Alabama College
Howard College
University of Alabama (3)
Woman's College of Alabama.

ARIZONA

University of Arizona

ARKANSAS

Arkansas College (3)
College of the Ozarks
Harding College
University of Arkansas

CALIFORNIA

College of the Pacific
La Verne College (3)
Occidental College (3)
Scripps College (3)
Stanford University
University of California
 at Los Angeles (3)
University of Redlands (1)
University of Santa Clara (3)
University of Southern California

COLORADO

Colorado Agricultural College
University of Colorado

CONNECTICUT

Connecticut Agricultural College
Connecticut College
Yale University (2) (3)

DELAWARE

University of Delaware

Women's College of the
 University of Delaware

DISTRICT OF COLUMBIA

American University
Catholic University of America
Howard University

FLORIDA

Florida State College for Women
University of Florida
University of Miami

GEORGIA

Brenau College
Clark University
Emory University
Georgia State College for Women
 (3)
LaGrange College
Mercer University (3)
Morehouse College
Morris Brown University
Oglethorpe University
Shorter College
University of Georgia
Wesleyan College

IDAHO

College of Idaho
Gooding College

ILLINOIS

Augustana College
Bradley Polytechnic Institute
Carthage College
Eureka College
Lake Forest College

Monmouth College
North Central College (3)
Rosary College (3)
St. Francis Xavier College
  for Women
St. Viator College (3)
University of Chicago
University of Illinois
Wheaton College (3)

INDIANA

Butler University (3)
Earlham College (3)
Evansville College (3)
Indiana University
Manchester College (3)
St. Mary-of-the-Woods College
University of Notre Dame
Valparaiso University
Wabash College (3)

IOWA

Central College
Coe College (1)
Iowa Wesleyan College (3)
Morningside College
Penn College
Trinity College
University of Dubuque
University of Iowa
Upper Iowa University (1) (3)
Western Union College

KANSAS

Bethany College (3)
Bethel College
College of Emporia
Friends University (3)
Kansas Wesleyan University
Marymount College
McPherson College
Municipal University of Wichita
Southwestern College (3)
University of Kansas (3)
Washburn College (3)

KENTUCKY

Asbury College
Berea College

Centre College of Kentucky
Kentucky Wesleyan College
Louisville Municipal College for
  Negroes
Transylvania College
Union College
University of Kentucky
University of Louisville

LOUISIANA

Centenary College (3)
Louisiana College (3)
Louisiana State University
New Orleans University
Southwestern Louisiana Institute
Straight College (3)

MAINE

Bates College
Colby College

MARYLAND

Goucher College
Hood College
Morgan College
University of Maryland (3)

MASSACHUSETTS

Clarke University
Emmanuel College (3)
Harvard University (2) (3)
International Y.M.C.A. College (3)
Massachusetts State College
Mount Holyoke College
Radcliffe College (3)
Simmons College
Smith College
Tufts College (3)
Williams College (3)

MICHIGAN

Calvin College
Colleges of the City of Detroit (3)
Emmanuel Missionary College (1)
  (3)
Hillsdale College (3)
Michigan State College of Agricul-
  ture and Applied Science (3)
Nazareth College

Olivet College
University of Detroit

MINNESOTA

Carleton College (3)
College of St. Benedict
College of St. Thomas
Concordia College (1) (3)
St. John's University
St. Mary's College

MISSISSIPPI

Mississippi College
Mississippi State College for Women
University of Mississippi

MISSOURI

Central College (3)
Lindenwood College for Women
Missouri Valley College
Park College
Rockhurst College (3)
Tarkio College
University of Missouri
Webster College
Westminster College
William Jewell College

MONTANA

Carroll College (3)
Intermountain Union College (3)

NEBRASKA

Doane College
Hastings College
Midland College
Nebraska Wesleyan University
University of Nebraska (3)
York College

NEVADA

University of Nevada

NEW HAMPSHIRE

Dartmouth College
University of New Hampshire (3)

NEW JERSEY

Brothers College of Drew University

College of Saint Elizabeth
Princeton University (2) (3)
Rutgers University
St. Peter's College (3)
Upsala College

NEW MEXICO

University of New Mexico

NEW YORK

Adelphi College
Alfred University
Colgate University (2) (3)
College of the City of New York (3)
College of New Rochelle
College of the Sacred Heart (2) (3)
Columbia College (3)
Cornell University
Elmira College
Fordham University
Hamilton College
Hartwick College (3)
Hobart College (3)
Manhattan College
New York University (3)
Niagara University
Russell Sage College
St. Francis College
St. John's College (3)
St. Lawrence University (3)
Skidmore College
Syracuse University
Union College (3)
University of Buffalo
Vassar College
Wagner Memorial Lutheran College (3)
Wells College

NORTH CAROLINA

Elon College
Guilford College
Johnson C. Smith University (1)
Lenoir-Rhyne College (3)
Livingstone College
Meredith College
Negro Agricultural and Technical College

University of North Carolina
Wake Forest College

NORTH DAKOTA

Jamestown College (3)
University of North Dakota

OHIO

Ashland College
Baldwin-Wallace College
Bluffton College
College of Mount St. Joseph-on-the-Ohio
Findlay College
Kenyon College
Marietta College
Mount Union College
Muskingum College
Notre Dame College
Oberlin College (2) (3)
Ohio Northern University
Ohio State University
Ohio University (3)
Ohio Wesleyan
Otterbein College
St. Mary's-of-the-Springs College
University of Akron (2) (3)
University of Toledo
Western College
Wilberforce University
Wittenberg College
Xavier University

OKLAHOMA

Oklahoma City University (3)
Panhandle Agricultural and Mechanical College
Phillips University (3)
University of Oklahoma (3)
University of Tulsa

OREGON

Albany College
Pacific College
Pacific University
University of Oregon
Willamette University

PENNSYLVANIA

Allegheny College
Bryn Mawr College (3)
Bucknell University (3)
Dickinson College (3)
Drexel Institute (3)
Duquesne University of the Holy Ghost (2) (3)
Elizabethtown College
Franklin and Marshall College (3)
Geneva College (3)
Gettysburg College
Haverford College (2) (3)
Lafayette College
La Salle College
Lehigh University (3)
Lincoln University
Marywood College
Moravian College
Muhlenberg College
Pennsylvania College for Women
Pennsylvania State College
Rosemont College
St. Joseph's College
St. Thomas College
Susquehanna University
Swarthmore College
Temple University
Thiel College
University of Pennsylvania
University of Pittsburgh
Washington and Jefferson College (3)
Westminster College
Wilson College

RHODE ISLAND

Brown University (3)
Pembroke College in Brown University
Providence College (3)

SOUTH CAROLINA

Benedict College
Coker College
Furman University
Greenville Women's College
Limestone College

Appendices

University of South Carolina
Wofford College

SOUTH DAKOTA

Dakota Wesleyan University
Huron College
University of South Dakota
Yankton College

TENNESSEE

Bethel College (3)
Cumberland University
Fisk University
Knoxville College
Lane College (3)
Maryville College
Tennessee Polytechnic Institute
Tusculum College
Union University
University of Chattanooga
University of Tennessee
Vanderbilt University

TEXAS

Abilene Christian College (3)
Baylor College for Women
Howard Payne College
Incarnate Word College (3)
St. Edward's University (1) (3)
Texas Christian University
Texas College
Texas College of Arts and Industries
Texas State College for Women
Texas Technological College
Trinity University
Wiley College (1)

UTAH

Brigham Young University

VERMONT

Bennington College
Middlebury College

Norwich University
University of Vermont

VIRGINIA

Bridgewater College (3)
Emory and Henry College
Hollins College
Lynchburg College
Mary Baldwin College
Randolph-Macon College
Richmond College of the University
of Richmond
Roanoke College
Washington and Lee University (3)
Westhampton College of the University of Richmond

WASHINGTON

College of Puget Sound (3)
Gonzaga University
Seattle Pacific College (1)
Spokane University (3)
State College of Washington
University of Washington
Whitman College (3)

WEST VIRGINIA

Bethany College
Davis and Elkins College (3)
Marshall College
Morris Harvey College (3)
Salem College
West Virginia University (3)
West Virginia Wesleyan College (3)

WISCONSIN

Carroll College
Lawrence College (3)
Marquette University
Milwaukee-Downer College (3)
Mount Mary College

WYOMING

University of Wyoming (3)

Appendix B

DATES OF ESTABLISHMENT OF DEANSHIP IN 319 LIBERAL ARTS COLLEGES IN THE UNITED STATES

(As reported by respective deans)

Year	Name of Institution
1870	Harvard University, Cambridge, Mass.
1871	Lincoln University, Lincoln University, Pa.
1873	Syracuse University, Syracuse, N. Y.
1876	Fisk University, Nashville, Tenn.
1877	Howard University, Washington, D. C.
	University of Pennsylvania, Philadelphia, Pa.
1880	University of Nebraska, Lincoln, Neb.
	University of Southern California, Los Angeles, Calif.
1881	Marquette University, Milwaukee, Wis.
	University of Detroit, Detroit, Mich.
1883	Princeton University, Princeton, N. J.
1884	Findlay College, Findlay, Ohio
	Haverford College, Haverford, Pa.
	Yale College, New Haven, Conn.
1885	Bryn Mawr College, Bryn Mawr, Pa.
1887	Catholic University of America, Washington, D. C.
1888	Morgan College, Baltimore, Md.
	Nebraska Wesleyan University, Lincoln, Neb.
	University of Kentucky, Lexington, Ky.
1889	Hobart College, Geneva, N. Y.
	Missouri Valley College, Marshall, Mo.
	St. Lawrence University, Canton, N. Y.
	University of Iowa, Iowa City, Iowa
1891	Carleton College, Northfield, Minn.
	Dickinson College, Carlisle, Pa.
	Hamilton College, Clinton, N. Y.
	Lenoir-Rhyne College, Hickory, N. C.
	Maryville College, Maryville, Tenn.
	New York University, New York, N. Y.
	Tufts College, Medford, Mass.
	University of Chattanooga, Chattanooga, Tenn.
1892	Goucher College, Baltimore, Md.
	Pembroke College (in Brown University), Providence, R. I.
	University of Chicago, Chicago, Ill.
	University of Kansas, Lawrence, Kansas

University of South Dakota, Vermillion, S. D.
1893 Bucknell University, Lewisburg, Pa.
1894 Dartmouth College, Hanover, N. H.
Indiana University, Bloomington, Ind.
Marietta College, Marietta, Ohio
Morningside College, Sioux City, Iowa
Radcliffe College, Cambridge, Mass.
University of Colorado, Boulder, Colo.
Wells College, Aurora, N. Y.,
Williams College, Williamstown, Mass.
1895 Cumberland University, Lebanon, Tenn.
Ohio State University, Columbus, Ohio
1896 Centre College of Kentucky, Danville, Ky.
Columbia College, New York, N. Y.
Cornell University, Ithaca, N. Y.
University of Missouri, Columbia, Mo.
Wesleyan College, Macon, Ga.
Western College, Oxford, Ohio
1897 Occidental College, Los Angeles, Calif.
1898 University of New Mexico, Albuquerque, N. M.
University of Vermont, Burlington, Vt.
1899 College of St. Elizabeth, Convent Station, N. J.
Kentucky Wesleyan College, Winchester, Ky.
University of Oregon, Eugene, Ore.
1900 Central University, Pella, Iowa
Kansas Wesleyan University, Salina, Kan.
Smith College, Northampton, Mass.
University of Georgia, Athens, Ga.
University of Nevada, Reno, Nev.
University of North Dakota, Grand Forks, N. D.
1901 Berea College, Berea, Ky. .
Elmira College, Elmira, N. Y.
Ohio University, Athens, Ohio
Rutgers University, New Brunswick, N. J.
Trinity University, Waxahachie, Tex.
Washburn College, Topeka, Kan.
1902 Adelphi College, Garden City, N. Y.
Clark University, Worcester, Mass.
Hastings College, Hastings, Neb.
LaGrange College, LaGrange, Ga.
Lindenwood College, St. Charles, Mo.
Ohio Northern University, Ada, Ohio
Simmons College, Boston, Mass.
1903 Baldwin-Wallace College, Berea, Ohio
Guilford College, Guilford College, N. C.
Lynchburg College, Lynchburg, Va.
Mount Union College, Alliance, Ohio
Texas State College for Women, Denton, Tex.

Transylvania College, Lexington, Ky.
University of North Carolina, Chapel Hill, N. C.
1904 College of New Rochelle, New Rochelle, N. Y.
Muhlenberg College, Allentown, Pa.
Otterbein College, Westerville, Ohio
Temple University, Philadelphia, Pa.
Vanderbilt University, Nashville, Tenn.
Wabash College, Crawfordsville, Ind.
Yankton College, Yankton, S. D.
1905 Carroll College, Waukesha, Wis.
Carthage College, Carthage, Ill.
Olivet College, Olivet, Mich.
Union College, Barbourville, Ky.
University of Alabama, Tuscaloosa, Ala.
University of Mississippi, University, Miss.
1906 Abilene Christian College, Abilene, Tex.
College of the Ozarks, Clarksville, Ark.
Howard College, Birmingham, Ala.
Lane College, Jackson, Tenn.
Meredith College, Raleigh, N. C.
Milwaukee-Downer College, Milwaukee, Wis.
Norwich University, Northfield, Vt.
Oberlin College, Oberlin, Ohio
Pennsylvania College for Women, Pittsburgh, Pa.
1907 College of Emporia, Emporia, Kan.
Furman University, Greenville, S. C.
Louisiana State University, Baton Rouge, La.
Massachusetts State College, Amherst, Mass.
1908 Asbury College, Wilmore, Ky.
Huron College, Huron, S. D.
Colorado Agricultural College, Fort Collins, Colo.
Tusculum College, Tusculum, Tenn.
University of Louisville, Louisville, Ky.
Washington and Lee University, Lexington, Va.
1909 College of the City of New York, New York, N. Y.
Lafayette College, Easton, Pa.
Middlebury College, Middlebury, Vt.
Moravian College, Bethlehem, Pa.
University of Oklahoma, Norman, Okla.
University of South Carolina, Columbia, S. C.
University of Toledo, Toledo, Ohio
Whitman College, Walla Walla, Wash.
Woman's College of Alabama, Montgomery, Ala.
1910 Agricultural & Technical Col. of North Carolina, Greensboro, N. C.
College of the Pacific, Stockton, Calif.
Jamestown College, Jamestown, N. D.
Florida State College for Women, Tallahassee, Fla.
Pennsylvania State College, State College, Pa.

Shorter College, Rome, Ga.
Texas Christian University, Forth Worth, Tex.
University of Florida, Gainesville, Fla.
West Virginia Wesleyan University, Buckhannon, W. Va.

1911 Baylor College for Women, Belton, Tex.
Elon College, Elon College, N. C.
Emory and Henry College, Emory, Va.
Mississippi State College for Women, Columbus, Miss.
Oklahoma City University, Oklahoma City, Okla.
Saint Mary-of-the-Woods College, Saint Mary-of-the-Woods, Ind.
Skidmore College, Saratoga Springs, N. Y.

1912 Clark University, Atlanta, Ga.
Dakota Wesleyan College, Mitchell, S. D.
Knoxville College, Knoxville, Tenn.
La Verne College, La Verne, Calif.
Morehouse College, Atlanta, Ga.
Morris Harvey College, Barboursville, W. Va.
North Central College, Naperville, Ill.
Rosary College, River Forest, Ill.
University of Arkansas, Fayetteville, Ark.
University of Santa Clara, Santa Clara, Calif.
Wake Forest College, Wake Forest, N. C.
West Virginia University, Morgantown, W. Va.
Wilberforce University, Wilberforce, Ohio

1913 Bluffton College, Bluffton, Ohio
Central College, Fayette, Mo.
College of Puget Sound, Tacoma, Wash.
Howard Payne College, Brownwood, Tex.
Morris Brown College, Atlanta, Ga.
Park College, Parkville, Mo.
Phillips University, Enid, Okla.
Spokane University, Spokane, Wash.
Swarthmore College, Swarthmore, Pa.
University of Akron, Akron, Ohio
University of Illinois, Urbana, Ill.
University of Tennessee, Knoxville, Tenn.
Vassar College, Poughkeepsie, N. Y.
Westminster College, Fulton, Mo.
York College, York, Neb.

1914 Albany College, Albany, Ore.
Benedict College, Columbia, S. C.
Duquesne University of the Holy Ghost, Pittsburgh, Pa.
Hood College, Frederick, Md.
Manhattan College, New York, N. Y.
Pacific University, Forest Grove, Ore.
University of Arizona, Tucson, Ariz.
University of Richmond, Richmond, Va.
Western Union College, Le Mars, Iowa

Westhampton College of University of Richmond, Richmond, Va.
Wittenberg College, Springfield, Ohio
Women's College, University of Delaware, Newark, Del.

1915 Brenau College, Gainesville, Ga.
Colleges of the City of Detroit, Detroit, Mich.
Louisiana College, Pineville, La.
Marywood College, Scranton, Pa.
Mount Mary College, Milwaukee, Wis.
St. Francis Xavier College for Women, Chicago, Ill.
University of Maryland, College Park, Md.
Xavier University, Cincinnati, Ohio

1916 Alfred University, Alfred, N. Y.
Emory University, Atlanta, Ga.
Limestone College, Gaffney, S. C.
Midland College, Fremont, Neb.
Muskingum College, New Concord, Ohio
Tennessee Polytechnic Institute, Cookeville, Tenn.
University of Delaware, Newark, Del.
University of New Hampshire, Durham, N. H.
Webster College, Webster Groves, Mo.

1917 Bethany College, Lindsborg, Kan.
Carroll College, Helena, Mont.
College of the Sacred Heart, Manhattanville, N. Y.
Connecticut College, New London, Conn.
Oglethorpe University, Atlanta, Ga.
Ohio Wesleyan University, Delaware, Ohio
Southwestern College, Winfield, Kan.
State College of Washington, Pullman, Wash.
St. Joseph's College, Philadelphia, Pa.

1918 McPherson College, McPherson, Kan.
Penn College, Oskaloosa, Iowa
Russell Sage College, Troy, N. Y.
Union University, Jackson, Tenn.
University of Buffalo, Buffalo, N. Y.
University of Notre Dame, Notre Dame, Ind.
University of Washington, Seattle, Wash.
University of Wyoming, Laramie, Wyo.

1919 Bridgewater College, Bridgewater, Va.
Butler University, Indianapolis, Ind.
Calvin College, Grand Rapids, Mich.
Centenary College, Shreveport, La.
Coker College, Hartsville, S. C.
Emmanuel College, Boston, Mass.
Fordham University, New York, N. Y.
Franklin and Marshall College, Lancaster, Pa.
Greenville Woman's College, Greenville, S. C.
Incarnate Word College, San Antonio, Tex.
Manchester College, North Manchester, Ind.

Providence College, Providence, R. I.
Roanoke College, Salem, Va.
Thiel College, Greenville, Pa.
Union College, Schenectady, N. Y.
University of Pittsburgh, Pittsburgh, Pa.
William Jewell College, Liberty, Mo.
1920 Brigham Young University, Provo, Utah
College of Mount St. Joseph, Mount St. Joseph, Ohio.
Evansville College, Evansville, Ind.
Gonzaga University, Spokane, Wash.
Lawrence College, Appleton, Wis.
New Orleans University, New Orleans, La.
Salem College, Salem, W. Va.
Upsala College, East Orange, N. J.
Wofford College, Spartanburg, S. C.
1921 Arkansas College, Batesville, Ark.
Augustana College, Rock Island, Ill.
Bethel College, Newton, Kan.
Friends University, Wichita, Kan.
Geneva College, Beaver Falls, Pa.
International Y.M.C.A. College, Springfield, Mass.
Randolph-Macon College, Ashland, Va.
Southwestern Louisiana Institute, Lafayette, La.
Straight College, New Orleans, La.
1922 Alabama College, Montevallo, Ala.
College of St. Thomas, St. Paul, Minn.
Davis and Elkins College, Elkins, W. Va.
Marymount College, Salina, Kan.
Notre Dame College, South Euclid, Ohio
Rosemont College, Rosemont, Pa.
University of California at Los Angeles, Los Angeles, Calif.
1923 Bethany College, Bethany, W. Va.
Bethel College, McKenzie, Tenn.
Elizabethtown College, Elizabethtown, Pa.
Eureka College, Eureka, Ill.
Intermountain Union College, Helena, Mont.
Lehigh University, Bethlehem, Pa.
Monmouth College, Monmouth, Ill.
Washington and Jefferson University, Washington, Pa.
1924 Earlham College, Richmond, Ind.
Harding College, Morrilton, Ark.
Marshall College, Huntington, W. Va.
Michigan State College of Agriculture, East Lansing, Mich.
Panhandle Agricultural and Mechanical College, Goodwell, Okla.
Rockhurst College, Kansas City, Mo.
St. John's University, Collegeville, Minn.
St. Mary's-of-the-Springs College, East Columbus, Ohio
St. Thomas College, Scranton, Pa.

University of Dubuque, Dubuque, Iowa
1925 American University, Washington, D. C.
Bradley Polytechnic Institute, Peoria, Ill.
College of St. Benedict, St. Joseph, Minn.
Doane College, Crete, Neb.
Georgia State College for Women, Milledgeville, Ga.
La Salle College, Philadelphia, Pa.
Livingstone College, Salisbury, N. C.
St. Mary's College, Winona, Minn.
Texas Technological College, Lubbock, Tex.
Wheaton College, Wheaton, Ill.
1926 Hillsdale College, Hillsdale, Mich.
Hollins College, Hollins, Va.
Municipal University of Wichita, Wichita, Kan.
Nazareth College, Nazareth, Mich.
St. John's College, Brooklyn, N. Y.
Valparaiso University, Valparaiso, Ind.
Wagner Memorial Lutheran College, Staten Island, N. Y.
1927 Ashland College, Ashland, Ohio
Gettysburg College, Gettysburg, Pa.
1928 Brothers College (of Drew University), Madison, N. J.
Hartwick College, Oneonta, N. Y.
Susquehanna University, Selinsgrove, Pa.
University of Miami, Coral Gables, Fla.
1929 Colby College, Waterville, Me.
Mount Holyoke College, South Hadley, Mass.
Scripps College, Claremont, Calif.
Tarkio College, Tarkio, Mo.
Texas College, Tyler, Tex.
Texas College of Arts and Industries, Kingsville, Tex.
1930 Colgate University, Hamilton, N. Y.
St. Peter's College, Jersey City, N. J.
1931 Connecticut Agricultural College, Storrs, Conn.
Gooding College, Wesleyan, Idaho
Lake Forest College, Lake Forest, Ill.
Louisville Municipal College, Louisville, Ky.
Willamette University, Salem, Ore.
1932 College of Idaho, Caldwell, Idaho
Mississippi College, Clinton, Miss.
St. Francis College, Brooklyn, N. Y.
1933 Drexel Institute, Philadelphia, Pa.
Kenyon College, Gambier, Ohio
Mercer University, Macon, Ga.
Westminster College, New Wilmington, Pa.